This handbook is loaded with invaluable
roll-out and develop your clean...

M000309407

A basic start-up business plan checklist	11 pages of invaluable references
5 fundamentals of business interaction	11 essential small cleaning tools & aids

5 cleaning services advertising examples, including a door hanger, postcard,
customer survey, flyer, website home page

Bidding formulas, overhead distribution formulas, price structure examples

Employment contracts, non-compete agreements, independent contractor
agreements explained, with follow-up references

6 fundamentals of customer relations	4 types of insurance your business may need

18 basic cleaning services provided by home cleaning services

15 basic cleaning services provided by janitorial services

What cleaning equipment to use, what it will cost and where you can purchase it

Work loading examples and production rate charts

How to determine a price or rate for your services

12 tips and techniques for negotiating your services

Where to find cost-effective employee background checks

8 factors employers must consider in determining employee or independent contractor status

Cleaning services classified employment ad examples

8 ways to motivate and help maintain employees

Where to find uniforms for a single employee or an entire crew

21 IRS tax forms, schedules and publications relevant to sole-proprietorships

5 tax structures to consider for your business

OSHA and DOL employer requirements that your business should be aware of

11 practical safety measures to help ensure employee and customer safety

8 essential cleaning practices to help build successful customer relationships

4 important facts regarding customer complaints that you should know about

10 gift and remembrance ideas to help improve customer relations

After you have read

Commercial & Residential Cleaning Services,

see the last page for information on ordering other Cleaning Services titles offered by THE KNOUEN GROUP,

such as this invaluable resource guide:

Cleaning Services Bid Estimation:
A Resource Guide To Cleaning Services Bid Estimating, Work Loading And Cost Accounting

Estimate workloads fast and accurately   **Calculate fair and competitive bid estimates**

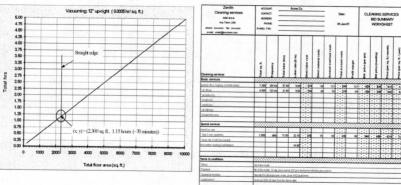

Rates or prices for cleaning services that are both competitive and profitable are typically based on accurate estimates for direct labor and materials, along with the applied overhead. Determining cleaning rates that are both competitive and lucrative is among the most important processes driving the profitability and success of any service based business.

CLEANING SERVICES BID ESTIMATION provides experienced professionals and aspiring entrepreneurs, with practical charts, tables and worksheets that can be used to determine cleaning times, production rates, price per square foot, work loading and other cost accounting endpoints, that are needed to establish cleaning services pricing or bid estimates. These tools, if used properly and consistently, can greatly enhance the profitability and competitive edge of Cleaning Services businesses. This guide comes complete with examples, supporting formulas, concise explanations and worksheet forms.

The guide is particularly well suited to individuals who have started cleaning services businesses recently and may be struggling with how to establish competitive service rates, as well as those contractors who are looking for ways to improve the profitability of their businesses. It is equally suited to those individuals without cleaning services experience, or those who are currently employed in the cleaning services industry, who are seriously considering self-employment as cleaning services contractors. They will find, that much of the practical information and many of the tools needed to make such a transition are presented herein.

COMMERCIAL & RESIDENTIAL CLEANING SERVICES:

A Resource Guide To Developing And Maintaining Your Own Janitorial Or Home Cleaning Business

First Edition

THE KNOUEN GROUP

Library of Congress Control Number: 2002109212

notice:

Table of Contents

Introduction (6)

1.)   The steps to a successful business (10)

2.)   Building a firm foundation (24)

3.)   Equipment & supplies (53)

4.)   Marketing and advertising (87)

5.)   Determining a price for your services (137)

6.)   Cleaning practices, safety and customer relations (205)

7.)   Insurance, licenses, taxes, hiring, etc., (234)

8.)   After the first reading (284)

9.)   Resources (290)

10.) Index (301)

Introduction

Congratulations! You've made the first important step towards starting your own full or part time cleaning business. This guide is written for aspiring entrepreneurs from all walks of life, wishing to earn extra income or build a lucrative cleaning service business.

Whether you are:

- *a student;*
- *recently retired;*
- *working full or part time;*
- *currently unemployed; or*
- *starting a second career,*

you will find practical ideas, techniques, and resources in this guide, to help you start a successful cleaning service business. The information found in this guide may be used to begin a:

- *janitorial service;*
- *home cleaning service; or a*
- *combined commercial & residential*

cleaning service.

In this guide you will learn about:

- *the steps to a successful business;*

- *how to determine the scope and direction of your business;*

- *what equipment and supplies are needed and where to find them;*

- *techniques for marketing, advertising, bidding and negotiating fees for your cleaning services;*

- *cleaning approaches and techniques to help you work efficiently, safely and maintain existing accounts;*

- *guidelines and techniques for expanding and maintaining your business; and*

- *legal and business requirements to consider, along with references to help meet them.*

Chapter 1

Four principle themes are threaded throughout this guide:

- *advocacy for the use of important, fundamental small business principles, guidelines and practices, such as preparing a business plan and the use of quantitative bid estimating methods, etc., wherever possible;*

- *the parallels between techniques and strategies that are used by professional athletes and sports organizations, to improve performance and enhance their chances for success, with similar approaches, that are quite useful, not only to cleaning services start-ups, but to many other small businesses as well;*

- *the inclusion of references to several resources for additional information on many important topics, in order to assist and encourage readers to research and explore further, the essential topics and factors, that may be critical to the success of their particular start-up;*

- *the emergence and importance of the internet as an almost essential tool, not only for advertising and promotion, but also for fundamental business research, on such topics as business planning, competitors, target markets, equipment, supplies, bidding, cleaning techniques, taxes, insurance, etc.,.*

Finally, this book is dedicated to:

• motivated persons, who have observed others succeed in starting their own business and wonder how they can get started;

and especially to,

• those individuals, who may have put forth great labor and effort towards starting their own businesses and perhaps through no apparent fault of their own, achieved less than desirable results.

Using the initiative and perseverance required to succeed at any endeavor, along with the instruction and resource references provided in this guide, you too may enjoy the rewards that starting your own business can bring.

The steps to a successful business

"The journey of a thousand miles
begins with a single step"
- Lao Tzu

The reasons or motivations for starting your own business are numerous.

- *Extra income*
- *A second family income*
- *Financial independence*
- *Dissatisfaction with the drudgery of routine jobs*
- *Freedom from the unreasonable expectations of managers or employers*
- *Flexibility in selecting your work schedule*
- *Starting a second career*
- *Supplementary income in retirement*
- *Control of your own financial destiny*

Whatever your reason or motivation, the important steps in starting your own business are:

- *believing that success is possible;*

- *developing a successful strategy or plan*;
- *setting attainable goals*;
- *taking action daily to achieve your goals*;
- *reviewing your progress and applying what you learn, to improve your business.*

Most us have learned of one or more of these concepts, or discovered them intuitively, at some time in our daily lives. We may have read about them, or heard them in one form or another, from parents, teachers, motivational speakers, and successful people from all walks of life. If we examine these steps closer, it is easy to see why each one is an important part of starting a successful business.

1.)   Believing that success is possible

"Success comes in cans; failures comes in can'ts"
- unknown

Clearly, we have little or no chance of succeeding if we do not believe in ourselves. From the very start, it will be "game over"! This is because we simply won't have the initiative to begin, or follow-through with a new endeavor.

"The difference between a successful person

11

and others is not a lack of strength,
not a lack of knowledge,
but rather a lack of will"
- Vince Lombardi

2.) Developing a successful strategy or plan

"a mediocre idea that generates enthusiasm will go
further than a great idea that inspires no one"
- Mary Kay Ash

Specific concepts and strategies for starting a cleaning business will be discussed in succeeding chapters, but first it is necessary to understand what a business plan or strategy is and why it is important in the first place.

The essence of any successful business plan or strategy can be expressed simply as **anticipation, organization** and **follow-through**. These concepts apply to virtually all businesses, ranging from a solo home based business, to the largest of corporations.

A successful plan or strategy **anticipates**:

- *the potential needs of customers;*
- *legal & business requirements;*
- *how to respond to change and remain com-*

petitive in the market place.

"... *chance favors the prepared mind*"
- Louis Pasteur

A successful plan or strategy **organizes**:

- *the use of the business's resources*;
- *the efforts of the business to meet the needs of customers*;
- *the efforts of the business to be competitive and grow.*

A successful plan or strategy ensures **follow-through**, by putting into action in an **organized** way, the components of the plan, based on the **anticipation** of both the customers needs and the competitive environment in the market place.

A simplified checklist for a business plan is presented in chapter two. Ideas and references on how to prepare specific elements of a business plan are presented throughout the book.

"*It is easier for a camel to pass through the eye of a needle if its lightly greased*"
- Kehlog Albran

3.) Setting attainable goals

*"The more I want to get something done,
the less I call it work"*
- *Richard Bach*

Setting attainable goals and achieving them, provides direction and focus to any endeavor. For example, those of us who have struggled with our finances, or our body weight at some point in our lives, have often experienced the most success in achieving longer term goals, by focusing on smaller goals.

Reducing the frequency and amount of discretionary spending, or reducing the size and number of snacks we eat, can provide immediate results or short term progress towards longer term goals, such as being "debt free", or having a slim attractive figure. These short term successes establish a basis for greater success and in turn, inspire us to focus on new goals.

For example, by achieving these initial short term goals, we may be further motivated to open a savings account, or take an exercise class and so on, until eventually, our long term goals are achieved. This is approach often holds true of starting a business.

The dot.com debacle of 2000 is at least in part, a case in point, for setting attainable short term goals in order to achieve longer term goals. Many failed dot.com start-ups, started with good ideas that may be profitable in the future, but simply failed to "look before they leaped".

A number of these companies, used virtually all of their start-up capital for marketing and infra-structure build-outs, to serve markets that had not yet matured. This was done in an effort to capture whole markets instantly. Clearly these companies would have been better served by conserving their capital and selecting shorter term goals. Specifically, they should have cho-sen goals more in line with the rate of accep-tance of the internet by consumers, as well as their access to it.

"An effort a day keeps failure away"
- unknown

4.) Taking action daily to achieve your goals

COMMERCIAL & RESIDENTIAL CLEANING SERVICES

> *"Eighty percent of success is just showing up"*
> - Woody Allen

Michael Jordan, one of the most famous sports figure of our time, and arguably the greatest basketball player of all time, was "cut" from his high school varsity basketball team as a sophomore. He responded by setting the goals of making the team in his junior year (a short term goal) and becoming the best player on the team (a longer term goal).

He enlisted the help of his coach, practicing drills everyday until he achieved his goals and the rest is "history", as they say. The point here, is that our goals can never be realized if we don't take action towards attaining them. Moreover, it is widely held that most successful people take an action most every day towards attaining their goals, doing so with almost singular focus.

> *"Some players dream of success
> while others wake up and work for it"*
> - *Unknown*

5.) Reviewing your progress and applying

what you learn to improve your business

"Failure is success if we learn from it"
                                        - Unknown

Its been said that "change is the only constant". Positive change in human endeavors often takes the form of continual improvement. Successful athletes perfect their sport through continual trial and error, often enlisting the help of a coach and training aids such as film or video tape, to review and improve their performance.

A successful business, like any other human endeavor is also result of the continual process of trial and error. If you remember the debacle of the "New Coke", then you are aware that even extremely successful companies, such as Coca Cola, are not exempt from this process.

Finally, another way of summarizing the <u>last four steps</u>, to starting a successful business, can be found in Shewart's **PDCA cycle** (**P**lan, **D**o, **C**heck, **A**ction). This concept is used by thousands of companies, worldwide, to help them improve the quality of their products and services. Note that the first step, **believing that success is possible,** is omitted in the diagram shown below, because the business is assumed to already exist. Notice that the PDCA cycle is a continual process for improving the quality of a company's products & services.

"Success is a journey, not a destination"
- Unknown

PDCA Cycle

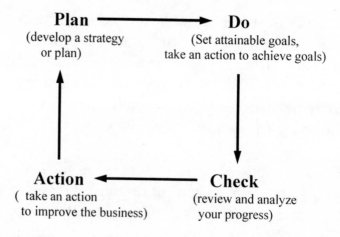

Plan ⟶ **Do**
(develop a strategy   (Set attainable goals,
or plan)   take an action to achieve goals)

Action ⟵ **Check**
(take an action   (review and analyze
to improve the business)   your progress)

This guide's scope & focus

In the preceding section we discussed principles that apply to the start-up of virtually any business. This guide is provided as an introduction to developing and maintaining a home based janitorial or home cleaning business. Levels of experience, skill sets and financial resources will undoubtedly vary among readers.

For clarity and ease of presentation, it is assumed that readers have only modest resources to work with and limited, or no experience with janitorial or home cleaning services. Readers with previous cleaning service experience and those with greater financial resources will also find useful ideas and references that will assist them in starting or expanding their own cleaning business.

Throughout the book, practical approaches and references will be presented, that provide direction for expanding a solo home based enterprise into a larger business concern. Many references in this guide are internet based. If you do not own a personal computer don't despair! Many schools, libraries, copy centers and coffee cafés provide temporary internet access for free, or at a nominal charge.

Persons affiliated with commercial cleaning services or franchises, should review their contract commitments, for any legally binding constraints, prior to starting a business of their own.

Those persons that are planning to start a cleaning services franchise, will find many of the resources presented in this guide helpful, in addition to any guidance they might receive as part of their franchise start-up kit or package.

If you are considering such an approach to starting your own business, you are strongly encouraged to consider carefully, the trade-offs between a franchise and an independent concern. For example, the name recognition, training and support that you may receive with the purchase of a franchise, should be weighed against the potentially adverse effects on your potential profit margins (e.g., franchise fees, loan repayments, royalties, etc.,). Moreover, some of these franchise expenses may be incurred indefinitely.

Some useful internet search pointers for beginners

Not all search engines take you directly to a website, if you type the address (e.g., www.xxx.com, www.xxx.org etc.,) directly into the blank field of the <u>search engine</u> text box, that is provided on your internet service provider's home page (usually somewhat below the browser's tool panel, or any where on the page below that). Nor will they necessarily return a list of links related to your topic.

Often, to reach your website destination, a valid website address must be typed into the internet browser's <u>file opener</u>, provided on the tool panel at the top of most browsers.

To ensure that you reach a website, you may first have to open up the file opener's pop up window and then type www.xxx.com, for example, directly into a blank field of the text box provided in the file opener pop up menu.

In some cases, you can just edit the current URL address, that is displayed in the text box field at the top of <u>every</u> browser, at all times and shows the <u>current</u> web address that you are at (at the beginning of each session, this usually the address of your internet service provider).

This is the text box that shows the prefix http:// at the far left of the box, followed by the website URL address that you are currently at, in your internet session. If you click into that box and it can be edited (a flashing cursor will appear in the box, if it can be edited), you can delete the current web address (i.e., every character to the right of the prefix http://), and type in a new website address, for the website that you wish to go to, just to the right the http:// prefix. Do <u>not</u> type in the parentheses that surround many of the internet addresses listed in this guide.

For example, http://www.xxx.org, or http://www.xxx.com or http://www.xxx.gov, etc.,. Then just hit return (sometimes, such as in the case of some Microsoft browsers, a "go" button is provided to the right of this text box). The complete address must be correct, with no remaining portions of the previous web address present.

Also, when performing searches using search

engines, be sure to read the "help" or "hints" provided. This will help you use keywords and phrases more effectively in your search. For additional information on the use of internet search engines and surfing on the internet, visit one of the many websites dedicated to this topic, such as **ww.w.searchenginewatch.com**.

The websites listed in this guide, were chosen because of their potential value to persons starting a cleaning services business. It is expected that a few websites will change their internet addresses over time, for one reason or another, or in some cases, cease to exist. Many websites that change their URL addresses, will use the old address as a virtual forwarding address, that will take you automatically to the new internet address. However, it is also possible, that the new website will not be found by typing the old URL address into a search engine.

If you cannot find a resource that is cited in this guide, during your search on the internet, try using searches with keywords or phrases, that are related to what the website might provide. More than likely, you will find a company that provides the same or similar products and services.

Chapter 2

Building a firm foundation

Determining the scope of your business

Even before you prepare a business plan for your cleaning business, there are a number of very important questions to consider.

Questions about the nature of the business:

- *Do I want to start a home cleaning business, janitorial service, or a combined service?*

- *What are the differences between each type of service?*

- *What is the potential market within traveling distance of my home?*

- *What resources are needed? Are they acces-*

24

sible to me?

Questions about personal preferences, personal commitment and resources:

- *Do I want to perform the services myself, or hire employees, or independent contractors?*

- *How much time do I have to invest?*

- *How much money (capital) do I have to invest?*

- *What is my availability to work days, nights, or weekends?*

Considerations regarding the nature of the business:

Ultimately, only you can answer the question regarding what type of business to start. Answering the question, **"What are the differences between each type of service?"**, can provide some insight, as to what type of start-up to pursue. There are some important factors to consider before answering both of these questions.

Focusing on one type of service (home or janitorial cleaning) may help conserve your start-up
resources. Alternatively, there may be a larger
potential market for a combined janitorial and
home cleaning service in the area where you
live, that may increase the chances for the
growth and success of your business.

Most janitorial work occurs predominantly in
the evenings and on the weekends, when many
businesses are not in operation. Conversely,
home cleaning or maid service often occurs during weekdays, or on weekends, when the client
is not present. One important exception would
be a hotel, or a bed & breakfast, where cleaning
predominates during the day after check-out, but
may occur around the clock.

**"What is the potential market within travel-
ing distance of my home?"**, is an important
question for most aspiring entrepreneurs to consider. **Suburban areas** are generally fertile markets for **home cleaning services**. If you live in a
suburb, far away from business zones/districts,
this may be the type of service to choose. If you

live in areas accessible to office parks or urban business districts, both of which are fertile markets for janitorial services, this type of service may be a "fit" for you.

What resources are needed? Are they accessible to me? Many of the tools and supplies for janitorial and home cleaning services are similar, but may vary significantly, depending on the scope of the service. On balance, a janitorial service start-up may require a larger initial investment for equipment and supplies, depending on the range of services offered (e.g., capital expenses for floor machines, or carpet cleaning equipment used in commercial floor care).

Considerations regarding personal preferences, commitment and resources:

Do I want to perform the services myself or hire employees or independent contractors? Here again, only you can answer these questions. If you have adequate start-up resources, you may wish to devote all of your efforts towards managing and promoting the business.

Eventually, in order for your business to grow, you will have to hire additional personnel. If you are new to cleaning services, or your start-up resources are limited, you may find that working new accounts initially, will allow you to refine estimates for labor, equipment and supplies and in particular, the time requirements for cleaning each account.

Accurately estimating cleaning times (i.e., sometimes called production rates when expressed as time per area), is often the most critical element in maintaining adequate profit margins, bidding contracts competitively and maintaining morale among employees. Additionally, cleaning new accounts yourself, will allow you to quickly correct any problems or inconsistencies with the service provided, (e.g., gaps in service due to a misunderstanding of the client's original requirements). Problems that arise early on in servicing a new account, should be resolved quickly to avoid losing the account.

"How much time and money do I have to invest?" and **"What is my availability for days, nights and weekends?"**, the answers to these questions are strictly personal choices. Your answers should be compatible with the type of business you are planning (e.g., part time, full time, home cleaning etc.,) and your current resources.

Regardless of the type of business you choose, it is important to remember that the old adage, "You get out of something, just what you put into to it.", remains true. It is well known that most successful entrepreneurs have worked long and tireless hours with single minded focus, in order to successfully launch and build their businesses.

Preparing a small business plan

Submitting a formal written business plan, is almost always a requirement to secure loans or investments, from anyone other than family members or friends. If you are thinking of taking out a loan to start your business, call a few lenders and ask them what their specific requirements are. Below is a checklist for a basic small business plan. It contains the business elements required by many lending establishments, for business ventures that present significant risks to the lender.

If it appears intimidating, don't panic! There's help. Instructional software tools, consultant contacts and examples of business plans may be obtained from a variety of sources to assist you in preparing your business plan, step by step. Some sources are listed below.

Resources for preparing a business plan

- **Small Business Administration's "The business plan road map to success" (www.irs.gov/smallbiz provides a link to a free downloadable PDF file)**

- **www.nolo.com (search for "small business" in the encyclopedia search engine)**

- **Business Planning Center (www.businessplans.org)**

- **www.bplans.com (provides planning tools and sample business plans)**

- **Yahoo! small business directory (search for "business plans")**

Basic Start-Up Business Plan
Checklist

1.) **Business scope and objectives:**
What is the name of your business? ____
Who are the principles? ____
(contact information for owners, managers etc.,)
What is the scope of your business's operations? ____
What are your business's services and the market share you hope to achieve ? ____

2.) **Products & services offered:**
What specific services you provide? ____
(e.g., home cleaning, janitorial, one-time cleaning and specific services as, vacuuming, carpet care, hard floor care, trash removal, window washing, etc.,)

3.) **Target market:**
Who you will sell to? ____
The reasons they need your services and why they will purchase them? ____

4.) **Critical factors for success:**
What is your financing (loans etc.,) ____
What is your cash flow (if any)? ____
What are your sales projections? ____
(usually given for 3 years)
When do you predict that you will break even? ____

5.) **Market plan/analysis:**
Who will your customers will be? ____
(e.g., for a home cleaning business: business executives, professionals, families where both parents work etc.,)
What are the pricing structures of your services? ____
(e.g., one time cleaning for an hourly fee, 3 times/week for a monthly fee etc.,)
How will you advertise and promote your business? ____

6.) **Break even analysis:**
Provide the specific information needed
to determine the break even point, including:
Start-up costs ____
Loan repayments ____
Operating expenses ____
Sales projections based on the number of accounts to be acquired (include also expected account turnover) ____

Calculations for breakeven ____
based on the total amount of sales needed to:

- *pay-off loans;*
- *recover start-up costs;*
- *establish a positive cash flow after operating costs.*

Important elements of a business plan

Every element of a business plan, is ultimately important and should be adequately researched. Then its description or summary should be written into your business plan, to reflect the specific goals and strategies of your start-up venture. The following discussion will illustrate how the principles of **anticipation, organization and follow-through** are applied to the development of a successful business plan.

Several business plan elements that bear discussion here, are:

- *company name/logo;*
- *business operations;*
- *market analysis;*
- *breakeven analysis.*

The selection of your company name and logo is important, for a number of reasons. First, your company's name & logo are its principle symbols of representation or recognition in the marketplace. They should reflect the objective(s) of your business and the needs of your target market, where possible.

Second, your company's name and logo should be unique and exclusive to your business. This means that before you make your final selection of a name or logo, potential candidates should be screened for the possibility of duplication or infringement.

For example, you could check sources such as the local phone company's yellow & white pages, state commerce SIC code books, internet search engines (e.g., Yahoo! yellow pages), etc., for potential duplication of company names. At the very least, ensure that you are not duplicating the name of existing businesses in <u>your area</u>. If you advertise outside your area, on the radio or internet for example, a more thorough check is warranted.

Several companies such as **www.legalname.com**, will provide domestic and global copyright and trademark searches for a fee (e.g., $95). You can also search for copyrights and trademarks on-line, at the website for the U.S. government office's for copyrights **www.loc.gov/copyright** and patents and trademarks, **www.uspto.gov**. Many businesses have suffered the loss of business, or experienced law suits due to infringement of another company's name or logo.

Finally, the name and logo (if used) should be:

- *short;*
- *to the point; and*
- *Memorable,*

if at all possible.

An excellent example is "**Your Final Janitorial Service**", the name of a janitorial service in Irving, Texas (**www.yfjs.com**), owned and operated by Richard and Mickie Moore. It is short, to the point and it is memorable. (note that the rights to this name may be protected by law)

Careful thought should be given to how your business will be structured and then run on a daily basis. In the beginning, perhaps the most important decision in structuring your **business operations**, will be whether and when, to hire additional personnel. This decision should be based objectively on:

- *the amount of start-up capital available;*
- *the number of existing or projected accounts, along with the time required to service them; and*
- *the remaining time left to devote to other aspects of the business.*

Other aspects of the business may include:

- *advertising and promotion of the business;*
- *bookkeeping;*
- *recruiting; and*
- *acquisition of equipment and supplies.*

All of these factors should be adequately considered and then your strategies summarized in your business plan. One very important aspect to consider, is whether to hire part-time or full employees, or independent contractors. Each of these choices, may have significant and far reaching effects on the profitability of your business.

For example, part-time employees may be exempt from some benefits afforded to full time employees by federal and state laws. Often these are costs which the employer must bear.

The criteria and burden of proof required by current U.S. tax laws, for declaring the use of independent contractors, must be considered carefully, before hiring them. Failure to meet these criteria, or to provide adequate records, could result in the back payment of payroll taxes (with compounded interest and severe financial penalties).

Using the principles of **anticipation, organization** and **follow-through**, in preparing a marketing plan, you will analyze the market place, and then:

- *determine your target market (who your most likely customers will be);*

- *determine the types of services you will provide (specific tasks to be performed, their frequency and pricing structures);*

- *determine how you will advertise and promote your business.*

Once the market plan has been completed, you

will have established your initial business strategies. Now you are nearly ready to begin implementing them, in an organized way that anticipates the needs of potential customers. All that remains, is to determine the essential legal and business requirements for your business. Some examples of these requirements are:

- *business licenses and permits;*
- *business and employee/contractor tax requirements (such as payroll taxes and tax reporting);*
- *OSHA safety regulations and reporting requirements;*
- *unemployment insurance (where applicable);*
- *workman's compensation insurance (where applicable);*
- *business and employee liability insurance and bonding.*

Your local chamber of commerce and the small business administration (SBA), are excellent resources that can assist you in determining these requirements. Tax lawyers, CPA's, and small business consultants may provide consultation as well.

A host of websites and books devoted to starting a small business are also available, to assist you in meeting legal and business requirements (see also, "resources for business planning", referenced earlier in this chapter).

Once you have determined the legal and business requirements for your business, you can begin to allocate your start-up resources such as capital, time and personnel, towards the implementation of your business plan. It is necessary to mention here, that the above approach is a preferred strategy. There are no restrictions, to implementing any of the elements of your business plan, in any practical sequence you choose, provided that you have the resources to do so and no laws are being violated.

Determining your target market, should be a matter of logic and market research for the area in which you live (or other areas you plan to market your services in). For example, if you are starting a home cleaning business, your market might consist of basic cleaning services for:

- **business executives;**
- **professionals** *(such as doctors, lawyers professors and engineers);*
- **entrepreneurs;**
- **working couples** *(with the necessary discretionary income);*
- **realtors** *("make ready" or "turnkey" home cleaning); and*
- **apartment managers** *("make ready" or "turnkey" apartment cleaning).*

Once you have determined your target market, you should immediately consider how you can reach these individuals, or establishments, in a targeted advertisement. For example, you might search the yellow pages for professional listings such as physicians dentists and lawyers in your area. You can cross-reference their home addresses in the white pages. Then you can mail flyers to these prospective customers, explaining:

- *the quality and uniqueness of your services;*
- *specific services that your company provides;*
- *discounts, specials;*

- *rates or prices (optional); and*
- *contact information.*

A twist on this approach, if you are providing both home and commercial services, is to send flyers to both the place of business and to the home residence of prospective customers.

If you are starting a janitorial service, your target market will consist of businesses and organizations in the area in which you live, or that you plan to market your services in. Small businesses and organizations such as:

- *professional offices (e.g., doctors, dentist, lawyers offices);*
- *schools, churches and civic organizations;*
- *small retail product & service businesses (such as branch banks, car dealerships, restaurants, hair salons etc.,);*
- *small manufacturing facilities or distribution warehouses;*
- *realtors ("make ready" or "turnkey" home and office cleaning); and*
- *apartment managers ("make ready" or "turnkey" apartment cleaning),*

41

comprise the typical clientele for a solo or small business janitorial start-up.

One way of developing a targeted advertising campaign, would be to drive through the area where you intend to market your services and write down the addresses of each potential business that you would like to have as clients. Then you can mail (or deliver in person), flyers with a description of services, tailored to each type of customer, along with prices (optional) and contact information, to each business.

Unless you have the name of the appropriate contact, you should address the mailer to the attention of the "responsible manager for janitorial or cleaning maintenance services". Calling each business, to ask for the name and title of the person in charge of janitorial or cleaning services, and then mailing the flyer to that person's attention, will allow you to further personalize and target your advertisement. You will also have references in the future, for any follow-up communications, or sales calls that you may make.

Many districts or locales in large cities, have dedicated business directories available from

your phone company or other local sources.
These directories may provide listings that are
more closely matched to the area in which you
plan to provide services. You may be able to
generate more selective mailing lists (and more
easily), from these directories than from a larger
metropolitan phone directory.

Determining and describing the type of services
you provide will depend on:

- *your personal preferences;*
- *the time you can to devote to cleaning accounts and managing your business;*
- *the availability of additional personnel;*
- *start-up capital;*
- *the amount and type of equipment currently accessible to you; and*
- *the type of transportation you currently have access to*.*

* Note: some floor machines are designed for disassembly and transportation in in the trunk of a small car, (e.g., see (www.centaur.machine.com)).

For example, you may not be able to transport
equipment such as floor machines, burnishers
and floor sweepers, in the vehicle(s) that you

currently have access to. You may need to contract out floor care services as needed, until you can afford the necessary transportation, etc.,.

Specific ideas for **types of services** to provide (and the language used to advertise them), can be found readily, in the yellow pages or on the internet. Searches for keywords and key phrases such as "commercial cleaning services", "residential cleaning services", "janitorial services", "home cleaning services", "maid services" etc., should turn up websites that can provide useful ideas. Listings of potential services for both home cleaning and janitorial services are provided here, to help you get started.

Typical home cleaning services

- *Vacuuming*
- *Carpet cleaning (steam, shampoo, or extraction)*
- *Dust furniture, base boards*
- *Polish furniture & appliances*
- *Empty waste containers & ash trays*
- *Floor sweeping*
- *Window sill & drapery dusting*
- *Window washing*
- *Wash & wax hard floors*
- *Clean bathroom and kitchen fixtures/appliances/ counter tops*

- *Make beds and change linens where linens are provided in advance*
- *Hang bathroom towels and refill tissue and fragrance dispensers (materials to be provided in advance)*
- *Clean out refrigerator*
- *Clean oven*
- *Empty or load the dish washer*
- *One time or deep cleaning (spring, pre/post move)*
- *Realtor "make ready " or "turnkey" cleaning*
- *Apartment management "make ready" or "turnkey" cleaning*

Typical janitorial cleaning services

- *Vacuuming*
- *Carpet cleaning (steam, shampoo or extraction)*
- *Dust furniture, base boards*
- *Polish office furniture & appliances*
- *Empty waste containers & ash trays*
- *Floor sweeping*
- *Window sill & drapery dusting*
- *Hard floor care (washing, waxing and buffing)*
- *Window washing*
- *Clean bathroom, kitchen or break-room fixtures/ appliances/counter tops*
- *Refill disposable towels, tissue, soap and deodorizers dispensers, as needed*
- *One time, or deep cleaning (pre/post move)*
- *Realtor "make ready " cleaning*

- *Apartment management "make ready" cleaning*
- *Grounds keeping or lot clean-up*

Determining pricing structures, is a mix of your personal preferences, your resources (particularly time and personnel) and most importantly, the expectations of your customers. Towards this end, you may wish to research cleaning service advertisements, or "cold call" other cleaning services and cleaning equipment and supply companies (many of their employees have run cleaning services of their own), in order to obtain ideas for pricing structures.

Here is an example of a price structure, for a janitorial cleaning service.

- *office size: 2500 sq. ft, 1 occupant/200 sq. ft*
- *services provided:*
  (vacuuming, emptying trash baskets, light dusting, cleaning bathroom & break room fixtures and floor sweeping)
- *cleaning time for one person: 1 hour*
- *frequency: 3 times/week;*
- *price: $375/mo*
  (note: for larger facilities with the same cleaning specifications, the price would be $0.15 per sq. ft)

- ***billing:*** *payable monthly*

Expectations for servicing and pricing structures, will vary greatly among clients and is often based on their present, or most recent experience with a cleaning service. Usually, a "walk
through" of the customer's establishment is performed. Then a "punch list" of specific services
(often room by room), is often prepared by the
contractor, as directed by the client.

The "walk through", is followed by a brief meeting with the client and a promise to deliver a
written quote. A verbal quote may be provided
on the spot, but should be followed-up with a
written quote, or a formal bid proposal and a service agreement or contract. This is a standard
approach, used by janitorial services to obtain
new accounts.

In the case of home cleaning, many customers
may also require a brief meeting with your company's representative. In this meeting you will
establish a relationship with the client. They
will outline the specifics, for what needs to be
cleaned, where supplies are kept (as applicable),
access to keys or security codes (as applicable)

etc.,. More discussion of advertising, pricing structures, and contract bidding will be provided in chapter 5.

Determining the breakeven point, in the case of a solo start-up, should be a fairly instinctive process. It is similar to making out your personal or family budget. In this case, you outline the total projected expenses, needed to start and maintain your business's operations, first. Then you determine the amount of sales revenue, projected over time, needed to equal the total amount of projected expenses. It is essential to have a good grasp of every significant expense that may be incurred and then to maintain detailed records, as they actually occur.

The components of breakeven analysis for the basic business plan presented above, are:

- *start-up costs;*
- *loan repayments;*
- *operating expenses;*
- *sales projections; and*
- *calculations for the breakeven point.*

Expenses for your business may include equipment and cleaning supplies, advertising, taxes, insurance, legal & license fees, transportation costs, rent (if you choose to expand your business from your home to an office), employee wages/taxes/insurance, contractor fees, loan repayments, office and communication expenses, etc.,.

Major expenses that you may incur initially, are:

- *licenses, fees, insurance;*
- *building leases (as applicable);*
- *utility deposits;*
- *cleaning equipment purchases & repair;*
- *office and communication equipment purchases & repair;*
- *vehicle purchases/ repair;*
- *initial ad campaigns*; etc.,.

These can be summarized as start-up costs in your breakeven analysis.

Once in operation, you will have daily or routine expenses, such as:

- *fuel;*
- *office supplies;*

- **communications**
  (such as pagers or cell phones, internet access);
- **utility bills;**
  rent *(as applicable);*
- **cleaning supplies**;
- **equipment repair**;
- **employee wages/taxes/insurance**;
- **contractor fees**;
- **advertising costs**; etc.,.

Once you have estimated or budgeted for these routine expenses, you can summarize them as operating expenses in your breakeven analysis. Loan repayments may occur routinely, or as significant cash flow is generated from fees that are collected from new accounts. They are treated as a separate expense category in the basic business plan presented here.

Sales projections should be realistic and conservative. They should be based on the size of the market in your area, the cost of advertising, competitive pricing structures and on the logistics and resources required to support new accounts, such as the time needed to service accounts, the cost and availability of manpower, equipment and supplies, as well as transportation costs and travel time. In a word, be "practical". For example, a fledgling, solo janitorial service, might set a goal to begin with, of securing at least one new account every 2 months, until the allocation of his/her resources and time constraints, "sparks" a need for additional help.

A fledgling, solo residential cleaning service, might set a similar goal of acquiring 3 new accounts every 2 months, until capacity is reached and additional employees must be hired. Whatever your goals or estimates for obtaining market share are, summarize them into the sales projections for your breakeven analysis.

Finally, a simplified illustration of your breakeven calculations may consist of, totaling projected sales revenues and then subtracting the total amount of loan repayments, the start-up costs and the total daily operating costs (accrued from the first day of operation, until the day of breakeven). When they total zero you have a projected breakeven point.

Breakeven point
expressed as a formula:

(total projected sales revenue) - (total loan repayments + total start-up costs + total accrued operating costs)= breakeven point

Actual calculations as practiced by accountants, will vary in complexity and how expenses and revenues are categorized, taking into account such factors as investments, capital equipment depreciation, taxes etc., but the principle is the same.

Even the most basic calculations will help to convey the strategies in your business plan and their chances for success. Your estimate of the breakeven point for your business, should be revised or <u>updated</u>, as changes in your business occur.

The ideas presented in this chapter, have introduced you to standard business strategies and planning for small business start-ups. They are "time honored" concepts, known for their ability to build the foundation for a successful business. Use them and profit from them!

Chapter 3

Equipment and supplies

In this chapter, various types of equipment and supplies used to start and maintain a cleaning service will be discussed. Some topics we will cover, are:

- *equipment requirements for specific clean-ing tasks;*
- *pricing;*
- *suppliers and alternative sourcing;*
- *equipment maintenance and spare parts.*

The objective of this chapter is to introduce the reader to:

- *basic types of equipment and supplies used to perform various cleaning tasks;*
- *typical pricing for equipment*;*
- *where to purchase equipment & supplies;*
- *tips on equipment maintenance and what spare parts/supplies to have on hand; and suggestions for essential equipment & sup-plies at start-up.*

* "starting prices" cited in this guide are approximate, actual prices will vary based on brand, model, features, quantity, supplier locale and rates of inflation.

Equipment for floor care

A detailed discussion of floor care systems (carpet or hard floor), is outside the scope of this guide. Proper professional floor care often requires specific knowledge about the type of material the floor covering is made from, as well as the sealants, coatings, or existing finishes (e.g., wax, polish etc.), on its surface.

It is equally important to know the appropriate cleaners, waxes, polishes or other surface treatments, that are compatible with each flooring material (e.g., cleaning solutions, shampoos, waxes, biocides, deodorizers, stain repellents etc.,). For example, cleaning solutions, waxes, polishes and other hard floor treatments can vary in:

* *suitability (ranging from unsuitable to best use); or*
* *compatibility (ranging from acceptable to*

potential for damage to the surface),
depending on whether the flooring is hardwood,
vinyl, polished stone or ceramic tile.

The proper application and removal of many
hard floor finishes or treatments (e.g., waxing,
recoating, stripping, buffing/burnishing), requires floor care expertise as well.

For example:

- **complete removal of existing damaged or
  dirty floor finishes** *(i.e., where the damage or
  soiling is beyond the point of a surface strip
  and recoat);*
- **uniformity of application;**
- **coating or finish cure times;**
- **buffing head pressure, rotor speed (RPM);**
  and
- **thickness and surface grades for scrubbing
  pads/ buffing pads,**

are often, important factors in producing a durable, glossy finish, that is free of imperfections
and in avoiding damage to the floor surface. For
instance, floor polishes and pads suitable for low
speed floor machines (~175–300 RPM), may not

be suitable for use with high speed burnishers/ spray buffers (1500-2000 RPM).

At a minimum, it is recommended that you re-search these lucrative specialty cleaning ser-vices, adequately, before attempting them pro-fessionally:

- **carpet care** *(shampooing, steam cleaning, bonnet cleaning, extraction and spot clean-ing); or*
- **hard floor care** *(application, buffing, or re-moval of floor finishes such as polishes, waxes etc., as well as routine cleaning).*

Inefficiency, poor quality of work, loss of busi-ness, property damage and liability, are all po-tential downsides to launching into a floor care project indiscriminately, or without proper train-ing or education.

For example, sloppy or excessive application of strippers and floor finishes, or applying them without proper "prep" work (e.g., furniture re-moval, taping floor moldings, or 'damming car-pet/hard floor interfaces with towels etc.,), can result in extra clean-up work or permanent damage to floor moldings, walls and carpets. Incomplete removal of many floor strippers, before applying floor finishes, can result in tackiness and incomplete curing.

This can result in furniture feet bonding tenaciously to the floor surface. Yellowing and rust stains and damage to the floor surface from the pulling action caused by furniture movements, can also occur. Replacing heavy furniture to their locations, before complete curing, can result in similar damage.

Often, the tenant, homeowner, or property management can provide information on the brand or type of floor covering involved. The floor covering manufacturer, or janitorial suppliers and floor care product companies can provide advice on the type of cleaning or polishing chemicals to use and how to apply them.

One approach that is useful when presented with a floor care request involving an unknown floor covering, is to ask for a sample of tile or a carpet square from the client, or the client's property management, which is often available and then take it to a local floor covering store for identification. From there you can identify a proper floor care system, through the floor covering store, or a janitorial supplier. Several resources are provided here, for floor care books, janitorial suppliers, floor care product companies and useful websites that may be helpful in your research of floor care technology and practices.

Floor care resources

- **Floor & Carpet Care**
  ($19.95 at 877-662-6905 or
  www.janitorbooks.com)

- www.hillyard.com
  (excellent instruction booklets
  available for use with their strip and wax
  and carpet care products)

- www.etcpads.com
  (has strip and wax guidelines on-line,
   for use in conjunction with their scrubbing
  and buffing pads)

- **Cleaning Schools 2000 and Beyond,
  Parts 1 & 2 (Carpet Care and Hard
  & Resilient Floor Care),**
  William Griffin, Perry Shimanoff
  ($25.00 each at Amazon.com)

- **Stone and Ceramic Tile Floor Care**
  free downloadable maintenance guides
  (www.aquamix.com or 800-366-6877 for
  technical assistance)

- **Hardwood, Carpet & Vinyl Floor Care**
  free downloadable maintenance guides
  (www.profloor.com or 800-281-EASY)

- **Floor Facts & Carpet Stain Guide**
  (www.bissell.com)

- **Chemical Information & Stain Guides
  For The Professional Carpet Cleaning
  Industry** (www.bane-clene.com)

- **www.cmmonline.com**
  (provides articles on cleaning & cleaning
  industry news)

- **Glossary of Hard Floor Care**
  (www.coastwidelabs.com)

- **IICRC and NAPC websites**

- **www.topfloor.com**

Carpet care equipment

Vacuum cleaners:

The most basic type of carpet care equipment
and no secret to anyone, is the vacuum cleaner.
Upright vacuum cleaners are usually the equipment of choice for routine cleaning of carpeted
flooring. Routine carpet cleaning removes dirt
and abrasive particles that contribute to a carpet's soiled appearance and eventually cause

damage to the pile/fibers/backing of a carpet. When placed under the same "continual use" conditions, encountered in a cleaning business, commercial vacuum models generally provide longer service than home models.

Hand held, manual carpet sweepers, designed for low pile carpet applications, are effective in removing large particles from the surface. They have the advantage of being quieter and are useful for spot cleaning, particularly where clients may be disturbed by noise. However, they just clean the surface and contribute only modestly to the carpet's appearance. Therefore, they are <u>not</u> considered useful, as a part of routine carpet maintenance (that is, deep and thorough cleaning).

The prices for vacuum cleaners ranges greatly depending on design and features. Prices start as low as ~$65, for light weight home units and go to several hundred dollars for commercial and specialty units. Vacuum cleaners that may be most useful to a solo start-up cleaning service are:

- ***upright vacuum cleaners*** *(starting at*

~$100);
- *light weight cordless upright vacuum cleaners (starting at ~$65); and*
- *portable vacuum cleaners with a swivel cart or shoulder straps, flexible hose and specialty brush & crevice attachments (starting as low as ~$150).*

Upright vacuum cleaners are the standard equipment of choice for most home and small business applications, as well as modular office settings found in large businesses. Light weight, cordless units are useful for quick spot cleaning and small areas that are inaccessible to electrical outlets.

Portable vacuum cleaners with proper attachments, are useful for narrow crevices, upholstery, draperies and irregular surfaces such as sideboards, window sills, crown molding etc.,. Portable vacuum cleaning units equipped with shoulder straps, are also sometimes advocated for use in conjunction with the latest "team cleaning" approaches, used by commercial cleaning companies, in the servicing of large commercial and public facilities.

Vacuum cleaners and the parts and accessories for them, can be purchased at vacuum cleaner manufacturer outlets, janitorial suppliers, electronics stores, appliance stores and department stores. If you are on a tight budget, you might search garage sales, flea markets and classified ads for bargains on used equipment.

Some considerations for purchasing and maintaining vacuum cleaners are:

- ***the motor rating*** *(horsepower and current);*
- ***the length of the electrical cord*** *(extension cords should be purchased regardless);*
- ***Special features*** *(bagless, beltless, HEPA filter action, dual motor, cleaning path, etc.,); and*
- ***attachments and spare parts*** *(replacement bags, belts, magnet guards/bars, roller brushes, extension cords & outlet adapters).*

It is a good idea, to consider having a <u>spare</u> vacuum cleaner (or to secure quick access to a loaner for use in an emergency). Malfunctions, due to belts breaking, brush rollers jamming and motors burning out are inevitable, even with the best of commercial units. A lucrative account may be in jeopardy, due to even a single failure to clean an important component of an account, such as the carpet. Roller brushes <u>will</u> wear down over time, reducing the unit's efficiency, to the point that it becomes virtually unusable, until the brushes are replaced. Critical items that you should consider having on location, or on the unit itself, are:

- *replacement bags (as applicable);*
- *magnet guard/bar;*
- *essential tools needed for belt replacement;*
- *replacement belts (as applicable); and*
- *extension cords & adapters (50 ft. or more, 3 prong grounded outlet adaptor).*

Making it a practice to empty the vacuum's bag or dirt reservoir <u>prior</u> to reaching full capacity, or as recommended by the manufacturer, can reduce "wear and tear" on the motor and will help maintain cleaning efficiency. Keeping the brush rollers clean and attaching a magnet guard/bar on the front of the unit, at carpet level (to catch paper clips screws & other metal objects), can also aid greatly in maintaining the unit's efficiency and will also minimize "wear and tear" on your vacuum cleaner.

Finally, as you expand your business, so will your resources and you will look for ways to improve efficiency and increase market share, and/or profitability. One idea to consider is a wide area sweeper (vacuum). These units have can cleaning paths from 24"-28" or longer. They also have a much larger bag capacity and handle larger debris more easily than smaller units.

They are ideal for large carpeted surface areas such as showroom floors and convention halls. These units can be purchased starting at ~$800 and up. Wide path automated floor sweepers offer a similar solution, to the efficient sweeping of large <u>hard</u> floor areas.

Carpet extractors & shampooing machines:

There are a wide variety of carpet cleaning systems used in professional and home carpet cleaning applications. Three of the most widely used types of carpet care systems are:

- *carpet extraction (hot water);*
- *carpet shampooing*; and
- *bonnet carpet cleaning.*

Hot water **carpet extraction** is one of the more popular carpet cleaning techniques because of its:

- *deep cleaning properties;*
- *its ease of use;*
- *drying times;*
- *wide acceptance by manufacturers;*
- *suitability to the fiber and backing composition of many carpets; and*
- *environmental friendliness.*

The carpet should be clean and free of obstructions or objects that may be damaged during cleaning. Usually, a single applicator is used to deliver a pre-spray cleaning solution, followed by pressurized delivery of a hot water cleaning solution and then immediate vacuum extraction of the "spent" or dirty cleaning solution.

The use of professional grade, neutral pH, low foaming surfactant cleaners, added in low concentrations, or as recommended by the manufacturer, is necessary to avoid leaving residues in the carpet, that can attract dirt later and to avoid damage to certain types of carpet fibers. Examples of incompatibility for carpet care treatments, are cleaners containing low pH cationic agents, such as bactericides and antistats, which are not for use, in caring for nylon carpets.

"Over wetting", may damage the carpet's backing and the underlying padding, as well as prolong drying times. Generally, the temperature of the water should not exceed 150F, to avoid damage to the carpet.

Carpet shampooing systems are often used in residential applications and work in a similar manner to carpet extraction, using shampoo cleaners. Bissell is one the leaders in residential & commercial carpet shampooing systems and equipment. Their equipment can be purchased, or rented in wide variety of places ranging from authorized factory dealers to supermarkets.

Bonnet carpet cleaning, usually involves the use of a moist or dry chemical cleaner dispersed over the carpet surface, followed by agitation, using a bonnet cleaner or floor machine, fitted with a special bonnet pad. The carpet is then vacuumed, to remove the cleaner along with dirt residues.

It is a useful technique that you may employ to save on equipment costs, if you are already using a floor machine for hard floor applications. Additionally, bonnet cleaning may be employed more frequently than other carpet care systems and has the advantage of minimal drying time. Its drawbacks are that it usually treats only the top of the fibers and for that reason, it is often not considered as effective as other cleaning systems.

Carpet extractors, shampooing equipment and bonnet cleaners, range significantly in their price, features, and suitability for a given application. Commercial, carpet extractors start as low as ~$800 and up. Self contained units start as low as ~$1200 and have a built in brush that scrubs the carpet. Less expensive steam cleaners and shampooing units start as low as ~$400 and are better suited to small commercial or residential applications. Bonnet cleaners or floor machines start as low as ~$600 and up. These units and the supplies for them, can be purchased at most janitorial equipment suppliers and many commercial equipment dealers, as well as some appliance and department stores.

If you select a carpet extraction system for your business, choosing a unit with adequate capacity for the cleaning solution & spent solution reservoirs, will improve efficiency and profitability. As with all of the equipment you acquire for your business, you should consider the pros and cons of purchasing demonstration models, or other used equipment, in order to conserve financial resources. Equipment rental, is also another viable option, provided you ensure the rental costs are adequately offset by your cleaning or floor care fees.

Hard floor care equipment

Floor machines & burnishers:

Floor machines are versatile machines, which are widely used for a variety of floor care tasks, including:

- **bonnet carpet cleaning** *(as mentioned above);*
- **cleaning or scrubbing** *(prior to the primary application, or recoating of buffable floor finishes);*

- *buffing (following the curing of a primary application, or recoats of buffable floor finishes); and*
- *spray buffing (used in the maintenance of relatively clean and relatively undamaged, buffable floor finishes).*

Floor machine prices start as low as ~$650. Pad diameter, rotor speed (~175-300 RPM) and head pressure, are features to consider when selecting this type of equipment. Classified ads and pawn shops are good places to look for used units, if you are on a tight budget.

Burnishers and **high speed spray buffers** are used to bring appropriately formulated buffable finishes to a high gloss. The gloss or sheen achieved, is sometimes referred to as a "wet look", because the floor still appears to be wet. They are similar to floor machines in operation, but run at much higher rotor speeds (1500-2000 RPM) and usually require specialized buffing pad attachments. Burnishers are usually powered by rectified DC current, battery packs, or propane. Rotor speed, pad diameter, head pressure and power capacity (i.e., battery & propane units), are features to consider when buying this type of equipment.

Some commercial burnishers have an advertised capability, for burnishing up 25,000 square feet in an hour. They are the "state of the art" in high quality hard floor care and can set your business apart from other janitorial services. Burnishers start as low as ~$800 and up. Propane Burnishers, with enhanced head pressure, start as low as ~$2200 and up. High speed spray buffers are a variation on a theme and deliver a metered spray in advance of the rotating buffing pad.

It is worthwhile here, to touch briefly on the basic steps in the application of a <u>buffable</u> floor finish (i.e., some floor finish formulations are "non-buffable" and are either not designed for, or do not respond to well to buffing).

New floors, which are treatable with buffable finishes, or a floor that has an extremely soiled, scuffed or degraded buffable finish, is a candidate for a primary application (i.e., a completely new floor finish) . The general steps are:

- ***removal of all furniture or obstructions;***
- ***Preparatory work, as needed*** (*such as taping off floor molding and "damming" carpet/*

hard floor interfaces with towels, etc.);

- *vacuuming or sweeping (followed by damp mopping, to remove all dust and loose dirt particles);*
- *removal of any existing finish with a stripper (formulated to remove existing finishes completely);*
- *neutralization and removal of the "spent" stripper (followed by rinsing and drying);*
- *cleaning of the floor surface with a neutral cleaner, usually at or near neutral pH (followed by thorough rinsing and drying);*
- *application of one or more coats of floor finish (each coat is thoroughly dried, and the areas that are irregular, or have thin streaks are "leveled"); and finally,*
- *the floor is buffed, or burnished to a final finish (often, one or more days later, after "deep", or complete curing has occurred).*

Commercial high speed blowers and floor fans are commonly to used to aid in the drying of carpeted and hard floor surfaces while they are being serviced. These fans can be a great help in reducing drying times and ensuring the completeness of drying, at various steps in floor cleaning processes.

Floor surfaces which have light scuffing, heel marks and/ or are lightly soiled, can be restored through a process of scrubbing and recoating.

The process is similar to a primary application, but instead of a stripper, a milder scrubbing formulation is used to remove a thin layer of the finish. After which, a "restorer" or recoat is applied and the floor buffed, or burnished.

Commercial hard floor finishing is generally outside the scope of a home cleaning service, unless a client has a significant amount of commercial grade hard flooring and wishes to have it professionally treated and cared for. Floor care for hardwood, polished stone and ceramic tile flooring, <u>not suited</u> to the preceding floor care system presented here, should be researched by the reader.

When in doubt regarding flooring types, or appropriate floor care systems, consult:

- *the client, or property manager;*
- *floor care equipment and product manufacturers; and/or*

- *janitorial suppliers, or commercial floor care specialists,*

in order to select the proper approach or system, as well as suitable equipment and supplies.

Brooms, dust mops, wet mops and bucket/ wringers:

Brooms should be selected for the appropriate application and floor surface:

- *smooth floors (bristles made with fine fibers);*
- *rough floors; (coarse bristles that can withstand the friction or drag on a rough surface)*
- *wet surfaces; (bristles made with synthetic fibers to avoid bristle softening and webbing of the broom's cleaning surface).*

Commercial grade brooms vary in price, depending on style, size and features. Push broom prices start as low as ~$10 dollars and up for 18" floor brushes and ~$20 and up for 36" floor brushes. Broom handles start as low as ~$5 and up.

Dust mops should have removable cleaning mittens or heads that can be washed or replaced. **Wet mops** heads should have "lie flat", cloth mop heads, that are of sufficient weight (e.g., 32 oz) and length, for the type of job and size of the areas you are cleaning. Its design should protect the floor surface from sharp or hard edges in its frame (as applicable).

A mop head that connects to the mop handle by means of a permanently attached threaded bolt, is often the simplest, most durable and reliable design. **Handles** for both broom and mops should generally be 60" long, in order to accommodate a range of users, or employees.

Bucket & wringer combinations should be selected in conjunction with your wet mop head selection, to ensure wringer capacity (i.e., it accommodates the size of your mop head). They should be of durable design and construction, for ease of mobility and be able to withstand the rigors of repeated mop wringing. A firm and adequate wringer action, at an ergonomic height and angle, are also important considerations that will promote efficiency and limit fatigue.

Commercial grade **dust mops and wet mops,** vary widely in price, style and features. Commercial dusters start as low as ~$20, wet mop heads start as low as ~$4 and are often available by the case. Mop handles start as low as ~$5. Commercial **bucket & wringer combinations** prices start as low as ~$100 and up, for a unit with 35 quart and 16-32 oz mop head, capacity. As with brooms, these are primary cleaning tools and appropriate thought should go into the purchase of these items.

A useful idea for institutional housekeeping and janitorial services start-ups to consider, once you have developed several accounts and have the resources, might be to keep a set of essential cleaning tools, such as brooms, mops & bucket/ wringers, janitor carts etc., at each account. This provides efficiency and convenience for you, or your employees, by saving time, in getting in and out of accounts.

Additionally, you may be able to subcontract ICs, or hire employees more easily, if for example, they need only provide their own vacuum cleaners. This also provides a potential selling point to the customer, who may use your cleaning items with your permission, for emergencies. Having said this, it is also a good idea, to request a secure storage area, onsite, with locks, that only authorized personnel can access. This will lessen the possibility for misplacement or theft of your property by the client's employees.

Home cleaning services may negotiate the use of certain items provided by the client, such as cleaners, mops, buckets, and vacuum cleaners. They may also offer a discount with the services they provide, for the use of these materials. In such cases, you should consider including provisions in your service agreement forms, in order to limit your liabilities for the use of a customer's equipment, i.e., failure or damage.

This may help you to conserve equipment resources, provide added efficiency in moving from account to account and help to limit the barriers for employment for some prospective employees. Regardless of whether you use the customer's equipment and supplies or not, an understanding relating to this practice should be established up front.

Basic cleaning equipment

Janitor carts, housekeeping carts, caddies:

Janitor carts, housekeeping carts, and **caddies**, are used to store and transport equipment and supplies, in and around the facilities that you are cleaning. They should be selected based on functionality, capacity and durability. **Housekeeping carts**, used in **commercial maid services** for hotels, nursing homes etc., are rated by room service capacity, based on the number of towel and linen changes that can be stored. Prices for housekeeping carts start as low as ~$500 for 8-10 room service capacity.

Janitor carts come in a variety of styles and sizes. A typical arrangement, is a cart that can accommodate a trash bag or can, mops/brooms, a bucket & wringer combination, cleaning solutions and small cleaning tools. Prices start as low as ~$130 and up, for these full featured carts. Variations on a theme, are trash cans on rollers, fitted with a removable janitor's caddy on its rim.

Mobile trash cans start as low as ~$35 and janitor caddies at ~$10 and up. Janitor caddy designs, include those that can be attached to a trash can or cart and those that are carried by hand. They are used for carrying small cleaning tools and cleaning solutions. Knowing the volume and logistics for trash removal at your accounts, will assist you in determining your needs for carts, caddies and mobile trash cans.

Some accounts will maintain these items in-house. It is often worthwhile to ask your client, what items (if any), are available for use by the members of your service. This topic may come up, if and when, you discuss where to store any of your own equipment or supplies onsite.

One idea that may useful for those beginning a janitorial service, is to purchase a general purpose dolly with a flat platform (similar to those sometimes used by movers). This can be used in conjunction with non-mobile trash cans that most commercial accounts will have onsite, to create a mobile trash can. These types of dollies start at ~$50. This is a great idea, for those with transportation that has a limited capacity for large items, such as a mobile trash can.

Its worth noting here, that the <u>ergonomics</u> of how you move your equipment and supplies "through" and "in and out" of a facility, as well as "in and out" of your vehicle, is an important consideration, that can:

- *greatly improve your cleaning efficiency;*
- *relates integrally to the cleaning strategy used for any given facility (e.g., the order in which tasks are completed); and*
- *affects the potential for limiting fatigue and unnecessary trips throughout the facilities that you clean.*

All of your equipment purchases should be made with these factors in mind. If you are unsure about the value, or utility of various pieces of equipment, clean a few different account using only the very basic equipment needed. Then formulate your purchases in light of your experiences and the logistics involved for cleaning all of your accounts.

Small cleaning tools and cleaning aids:

Other types of equipment that are very useful

and quite often are essential, includes but is not limited to:

- *wand, or feather dusters;*
- *hand brushes;*
- *toilet bowl brushes;*
- *toilet plunger;*
- *hand and floor squeegees,*
- *putty knifes and box cutters;*
- *a small compliment of screwdrivers, wrenches and pliers;*
- *dust cloths, buffing cloths, wet cloths and scouring pads;*
- *utility spray bottles and basic cleaning solutions;*
- *safety signs/pylons, non-porous gloves and eye protection*
- *tape measure.*

Most of these items, start at less than ~$5. **Safety signs and pylons** start at ~$20 and up. Generally, signs and pylons should be plainly visible at distances of ~30 ft, where possible. **Putty knives** are handy for removing gum from floors etc.,. **Hand and floor Squeegee** prices start as low as ~$10. These are an important job aids, for such tasks as, window/mirror cleaning,

cleaning up excess liquid from spills and in, bulk removal of "spent" floor stripping solutions used in floor care treatments. A **tape measure** is useful for estimating floor areas.

Spray bottles are used as cleaning and rinse solution applicators. Considerable savings can be achieved, by mixing your own cleaning solutions from concentrates. Basic cleaning solutions to consider, are:

- *window and mirror cleaners;*
- *neutral pH, general purpose floor cleaners;*
- *specialty cleaners for bathroom fixtures;*
- *specialty cleaners for furniture;*
- *general purpose spot cleaners for carpets;*
- *multipurpose cleaners and degreasers;*
- *disinfectant cleaners.*

Supplies provided to the customer

Housekeeping supplies, that are sometimes provided by cleaning services to the customer, is a subject that bears discussion here. This is an important consideration for janitorial services and institutional housekeeping services. Many large public and private facilities, frequently require

81

this additional service.

Many janitorial services and maid services will provide housekeeping supplies, as part of the services they provide. For example, you may have a service agreement to provide bathroom supplies such as toilet tissue, sanitary toilet seat covers, feminine care products, paper towels, deodorizers, soaps, urinal cakes/guards, dispensers etc.,. You might also be contracted to supply housekeeping supplies such as trash liners, paper toweling, napkins, safety kits etc.,.

Pricing for these items, as with your equipment, will vary with their features, quality and the volume, in which you purchase them. Just as often as not and for a variety of reasons, the customer may wish to control some, or all these expenses in-house. Nevertheless, you should be prepared to address this issue with prospective clients.

In the event that you are unable to provide these supplies yourself (or you simply decide that it is outside the scope of your business), be prepared to offer cost effective suggestions for:

- *what type of items offer the best function or features;*
- *relative pricing;*

- *where to purchase them.*

This will go a long way towards accommodating your client's needs and in establishing credibility. You may also earn a reputation as a <u>problem solver</u>, if for example, you suggest the use of superior soap dispensers, that actually dispense on command and don't drip after dispensing! Or you may suggest a different type of disposable paper towel system that ensures reliable and cost effective disposable towel usage and so on.

Some thought should be given, to accepting the responsibility for providing supplies to your customers. Some factors to consider, are:

- *accurate estimates for supply usage, and appropriate solutions to address significant or unexpected fluctuations in usage;*

- *the additional time and resources required for purchasing, transporting and tracking the usage of your customers' supplies;*

- *the "mark-up" (if any) that you will charge for the service and the applicable local and state sales tax laws in your state.*

One idea that may make sense for your business, is to make customers an offer to provide items, such as trash liners for free, in exchange for adding an additional specialty service, such as a weekly or monthly window cleaning, or a quarterly floor waxing service. In this way, you can provide something for free to the customer and more than recoup your costs for the trash liners. Trash liners are usually, quite predictable in terms of usage and they are easy to transport from facility to facility.

Keeping a supply of your own trash liners for emergencies, or offering to provide trash liners to your clients at cost, or for free, will give you greater control in complying with cleaning specifications. Clients may occasionally forget to replenish their housekeeping supplies and if you cannot reuse the liners, you may find yourself in a bind. Even if the facility contact understands why liners are reused or missing, or worst case, the trash is not emptied at all (this option should be avoided, if at all possible), other employees may not be aware of the problem. Many of them will register their dissatisfaction immediately, or sometime in the future. This could seriously erode your company's reputation and put the account in jeopardy.

A list of some janitorial equipment and janitorial supply websites is provided here, in order to help you educate yourself to the variety of pricing and features for the equipment & supplies discussed in this chapter. This list, is by no means exhaustive and no endorsement, written or implied is made regarding the products and services they provide.

Finally, it is a very good idea to speak with experienced sales persons, at one or more janitorial equipment suppliers, regarding a product's suitability to your applications, before you purchase it. They usually will be more than glad to help you with your needs.

Janitorial equipment and supply websites

- www.cleanking.com

- www.janitorialsuppliesstore.com

- www.jani-mart.com

- www.fishmansupply.com

- www.1st-janitorial-equipment-and-supplies.com

- www.cleanproindustries.com

- www.coastalpapersupply.com

- www.cleaning-equipment.com

- www.centaur.machines.com

- www.nycoproducts.com

- www.janitorshop.com

- www.bigtray.com

- www.cyberclean.com

Chapter 4

Marketing and advertising

In chapter two, we discussed essential factors to consider in preparing a marketing plan. Specifically, we discussed some examples of how you might:

- *determine your target market (i.e., who your most likely customers, will be);*

- *determine the types of services that you will provide (i.e., specific tasks to be performed, their frequency and pricing structures);*

- *determine how you will advertise and promote your business.*

In this chapter, we will expand our discussion of marketing to include:

- *additional ideas on determining target markets;*

- *effective strategies for advertising and pro-*

moting your business.

Determining your target markets

Customer needs and discretionary spending

In chapter two, we listed several examples of typical clientele, for a home cleaning service and for a solo, or small, janitorial service:

Typical clientele for a home cleaning Business:

- *business executives*;
- *Professionals (such as doctors, lawyers and engineers);*
- *entrepreneurs*;
- *working couples (with the necessary discretionary income);*
- *realtors ("make ready" or "turnkey" home cleaning); and*
- *apartment managers ("make ready" or "turnkey" apartment home cleaning).*

Typical clientele for a small janitorial service:

- *professional offices (e.g., doctors, dentists, and lawyer's offices);*
- *schools, churches and civic organizations;*
- *small retail product & service businesses (such as branch banks, car dealerships, restaurants, hair salons etc.,);*
- *small manufacturing facilities or distribution warehouses;*
- *realtors ("make ready" or "turnkey" home and office cleaning); and*
- *apartment management ("make ready" or "turnkey" apartment cleaning).*

Prospective customers for both home cleaning and janitorial services, all have at least one of two things in common:

- *limited resources to do their own cleaning (e.g., time or personnel);*

- *a desire or need to focus their time, money, and energies on other activities.*

Another thread that unites all of your prospective customers is <u>discretionary spending</u>. For example, an otherwise busy husband, may enlist the services of a local maid service, to make his residence more presentable, before his wife returns from a two week long business trip. The plant manager of a manufacturing company may order special "one time" floor care services, in order to enhance the image of his facility, prior to an important business meeting, or a plant tour for customers, or corporate executives.

Discretionary spending, is an especially important factor for home cleaning businesses to consider, when determining target markets and developing advertising strategies. While most working people can afford at least some form of residential cleaning services, affluent people have greater discretionary income and are often, more likely to engage the services of a home cleaning business. For example, if you are distributing flyers to promote your company's home cleaning services, you might target:

- *homes in affluent subdivisions or townhouse communities;*
- *luxury apartment complexes;*
- *parking lots at social events (i.e., classical music concerts, art museum exhibits, busi-*

ness or trade conventions, church services in affluent neighborhoods etc.,);

- **public access bulletin boards in affluent communities** *(e.g., local libraries, launderettes, apartment clubhouses, meeting halls etc.,).*

Flyers are one of the cheapest, most accessible and direct forms of print advertising. They are useful for promoting home cleaning and janitorial services. You can prepare a one page advertisement at home, on a computer, in an hour or less. With a PC and a printer (with adequate toner capacity, e.g., 1500 pages per cartridge), you can make your own flyers for as little as:

- *~6 cents per flyer;*
- *~$6 per 100 flyers; or*
- *~$60 per 1000 flyers.*

You may also prepare your flyer at many schools, libraries and copy centers, where they provide temporary access to a personal computer or word processor, for a nominal fee. Copiers are usually available as well, so that you can make inexpensive copies for distribution.

There are also many print advertising and re-sume´ services, that will prepare your flyer for you and provide copies for a fee.

One worthwhile technique to employ in preparing your flyer, is to use both sides of the flyer to your fullest advantage. The first step is to get the reader's attention. After you have the reader's attention, the flyer should provide adequate information, to answer common questions that may arise in the reader's mind, as they glance over it. The <u>fewer unanswered questions</u> that the reader is left with, the <u>more accessible</u> your service becomes to them and the greater the chances, that they will contact you.

For example, you can use the front of the flyer to:

- *catch the attention of the reader;*
- *describe how your services will benefit the reader;*
- *provide contact information; and*
- *list the communities that your company serves (cities, boroughs, zip codes, etc.,).*

You can then use the back of the flyer to provide detailed information about:

- *specific services that your business provides;*
- *rates or price structures;*
- *how to set up a meeting with your representative and what type of consultation will be provided;*
- *key release, sign-off instructions;*
- *bonding & insurance information,* etc.,.

An example of a flyer for a home cleaning service is provided here, in order to give you some ideas for developing your own flyer. The cleaning service company in this example, provides details and pricing information for a "basic cleaning package". If you use ledger sized paper (i.e., 8 1/2" x 14"), or a smaller type font, you may be able to include additional information on special services in your flyer.

If you have worked for other cleaning services before, include the number of years of experience that you have in the industry. If you are using them exclusively, include a statement, to the effect that you use only biodegradable cleaners. You may also want to consider, an offer to provide references upon request, in order to help establish trust and credibility. Many of your existing customers will be happy to acknowledge the quality of your company's services.

The approach for preparing a flyer for a janitorial service is much the same. However, it should be noted that the scope and the scale of commercial customers' needs vary widely. For that reason, most commercial cleaning services use flyers, to invite potential customers to call, for free estimates, or to receive an onsite consultation, rather than providing price quotes.

If you are using a flyer to advertise a commercial maid service or janitorial service, as a "teaser", you might offer discounts on special, "one time", or introductory, services. For example, you could advertise 20% off on a "one time" carpet extraction, or "strip and refinish" service, to those customers who hire you for their routine cleaning needs.

It's a good idea, if you must quote prices in commercial cleaning advertisements, to provide these quotes as <u>rates</u> based on such criteria as, per 100 sq. ft. of office space, cleaning frequency, room or building square footage etc.,.

When quoting a fixed price, you should use qualifiers, such as an alternate or additional rate, that would apply for rooms exceeding a maximum size. This will help to ensure that you have control over your profit margins, regardless of the size, or difficulty of the job.

Perhaps the best use of a flyer, in conjunction with promoting a commercial cleaning service, is to use it as a means of introducing of your cleaning service, to new businesses, opening in areas that you are already serving (e.g., strip mall grand openings), or to all potential customers, in areas that you are expanding your cleaning services to.

Let these customers know that you are eager to serve their needs, with unique, cost effective solutions and reliable service. Include some type of introductory service special, to provide an added incentive for potential customers needing that service, to contact you.

Flyers can be sent to existing customers, to alert them to specials and expanding services. This can help to increase revenue from existing accounts.

ATTENTION!

ACME CLEANING, INC.

Provides professional cleaning services for apartments and homes, tailored to your needs !!!

Enjoy <u>more free time</u>, to do the things you really want to do!!!

Present this ad, to receive $5.00 off your initial "basic service" cleaning

Acme Cleaning Service, Inc.
Servicing: Anytown, USA
Owner: Your Name
Phone: xxx-xxx-xxxx
Cellular/pager: xxx-xxx-xxxx
Fully Bonded & Insured by: SZERLIP & CO
Member NAPC

Visit our website
(www.acme-cleaning.com)
or
See our ad in the yellow pages

(Please read the backside of this flyer for for pricing and order information)

Acme Cleaning, Inc.
Basic Service

Bathroom
- Bathtub
- Toilet
- Sink
- Mirror
- Sweep & mop floor
- Empty trash

Kitchen
- Counters
- Outside cabinets
- Appliances
- Sweep & mop floor
- Empty trash

Bedroom
- Make bed
- Vacuum, or
- Sweep & mop floor
- Furniture dusting
- Empty trash

Please call for information & rates on all of our services, or to obtain a free quote for customized service plans.

Living Area
- Vacuum, or
- Sweep & mop floor
- Furniture dusting
- Empty trash

Payment Methods: (check or cash)
- prepay;
- pay at completion of service; or
- leave cash or check in a visible spot (for customers using key release sign-off forms);
- $25 return fee for bad checks.

Subtract $5 for an initial clean with this flyer!

Basic Service pricing:
1 bed 1 bath: weekly - $20, Biweekly - $30, initial - $50
2 bed 1 bath :weekly - $25, Biweekly - $35, initial - $55
3 bed 2 bath: weekly -$35, Biweekly - $45, initial - $65
(add $5 for each extra bedroom, bath or living area)

Owner: Your Name
Phone: xxx-xxx-xxxx   cellular/pager: xxx-xxx-xxxx
E-mail: e-mail@acme-cleaning.com

Target markets, for a commercial cleaning business are often determined by the specific needs of the customer. For example, businesses or organizations that have a lot of customer traffic, such as:

- *banks;*
- *restaurants;*
- *convenience stores/ markets;*
- *car dealerships;*
- *hair salons;*
- *medical & dental practices*, etc.,

have a <u>critical need</u> to maintain bright and spotlessly clean environments, in order to help ensure a pleasant shopping experience or business environment, maintain professional credibility and to attract repeat business, as applicable.

Advertisements, as with direct person to person solicitations, should communicate an <u>understanding</u> of the specific needs of your customer, provide assurances of professional services at competitive rates and as warranted, offer unique solutions that meet the needs of your customer base. Providing unique and effective solutions that meet the needs of customers, will help to differentiate you from your competition and improve the chances for long term business relationships.

Businesses with a great deal of customer traffic, often require a <u>higher cleaning frequency</u>, in order to maintain them adequately. They are also fertile ground for the sale of specialty services, that are needed to maintain or improve the appearance of their establishments, such as carpet extraction, floor stripping & refinishing, window cleaning and exterior pressure washing.

A successful business manager will recognize how critical the appearance of their establishment is and will ensure that routine and special services are performed, as frequently as needed. Consequently, he or she is more likely to be receptive to a targeted advertisement, that highlights your business's specialty services, or your company's availability for <u>daily</u> cleaning and maintenance.

Commercial property management services and residential realty or apartment managers, usually will have a standard set of cleaning tasks in mind for "turnkey" or "make ready" services and often, they may have a need, or requirement, for flexibility in scheduling and for quick turn-around times.

Alternatively, other businesses, such as distribution warehouses, small manufacturing facilities, etc., may simply require a neat and sanitary environment for their employees to work in.

These businesses are likely to be most interested in:

- *basic cleaning services;*
- *competitive prices;*
- *reliability and punctuality,*

when choosing their cleaning service company.

The cleaning frequency for these types of businesses, is often lower, than for businesses with a lot of onsite customer traffic. The cleaning frequency may be driven, solely by the number of employees working in office environments and the amount and type of business activities, or the level of employee traffic, requiring routine cleaning. In the case of "turnkey" or "make ready" cleaning services, tenant turnover will be the main driver for cleaning frequency.

Once you have successfully secured one or more accounts, from among the various types residential customers or businesses described above, you will begin to see first hand, how you can translate your knowledge of your current customer's needs and discretionary spending, into even more skillful and refined advertisements and solicitations. This in turn, will help you to attract more business from residential customers with similar profiles, or commercial customers engaged in similar or identical businesses.

Additionally, you can reference the experience you gain, for each <u>new type</u> of customer that you establish business with, in future advertisements and direct solicitations. As your understanding in serving the needs of each type of customer grows and you continue to refine your promotional strategies, these customer bases will eventually evolve into niche markets for your company.

Assessing the competition

The cleaning service industry, as with most service based industries, is very competitive. In order for your business to launch successfully and flourish, you must know something about:

- *who your competition is;*
- *what their products and services are;*
- *what their resources and market share are;*
- *what their strategies are; and*
- *how you will use your skills and assets to compete initially and then maintain a competitive advantage.*

You should make a point of learning as much as you can about the "Who, what and why?", of your competition. At first, while formulating your own start-up strategies and then periodically, as you launch and expand your business.

To do this, you should research print media, such as the local yellow pages, newspaper classifieds, as well as internet directories and search engines, for competing cleaning businesses in your area. One internet source that may be helpful is the **National Association of professional cleaners (NAPC)**. You can locate all of their registered members by registering yourself for $25 at **www.cleaningassociation.com**. Look closely at

the advertisements and websites of your competitors for clues and answers to:

- *what services they provide;*
- *what prices, rates or specials they advertise;*
- *what promises or guarantees they make;*
- *what their experience and credentials are;*
- *how they are trying to attract customers;*
- *how they are trying to distinguish themselves from their competition;*
- *what they say or imply about their competition;*
- *what their size is (e.g., number of employees,
  scope of services provided).*

This research will prove invaluable, as you plan
your advertising and marketing strategies. It
should also inspire you, to think of ideas on how
to distinguish your business from the competition.

General, or core service industry themes, that
will undoubtedly emerge, from researching your
competitors' advertising, are:

- *quality of service;*
- *competitive rates;*

- *reliability and punctuality;*
- *experienced, professional and courteous service;*
- *service guarantees;*
- *a wide range of standard services suited to the customer's needs;*
- *specialized or customized services;*
- *employees are bonded and insured.*

Other approaches for learning about your competition, that can be effective and should be noted, are:

- *networking among friends, relatives, acquaintances, and business owners/ managers, that you come into contact with;*

- *"cold calling" the competition for information on the types of services and rates that they charge;*

- *"cold calling" potential customers for data on the specific types of services they are using and the rates that they are paying;*

- *distributing a customer survey via postcards, or flyers.*

When you employ the networking approach, you should garner or obtain pertinent details where applicable. For instance, details such as the size of the establishment or residence, the number employees or occupants, or the number of bedrooms, offices, bathrooms etc., as well as the frequency and types of cleaning services provided, are important factors in putting service rates or prices in perspective. You may be surprised what you can learn with the right sources.

If you decide to "cold call" a <u>small</u> sampling of competing cleaning services, you should consider working from a script of questions and provide fairly detailed cleaning scenarios, in order to side step an invitation for an onsite consultation and in order to obtain more accurate information. The "barriers to access" for specific information may be significant. Asking short, targeted questions, will be your best bet, for extracting meaningful information.

For example, you can ask cleaning services, what the approximate rates are, for their specialized or basic cleaning services, based on specific input that you provide, such as building square footage, the number of carpeted rooms, bathrooms, number of occupants, cleaning frequency etc.,. It goes without saying that you should be brief, courteous and refrain from leading the competitor's representative on, maliciously. Always observe the golden rule and ask only for the general range of your competitors' service rates.

A variation on this approach, is to "cold call" a small sampling of the types of businesses, that you eventually intend to solicit business from. In order to remain anonymous, a slight "stretch", would be to say that you are with a marketing firm, representing a cleaning service in the area.

Before you place any calls, you should have an idea as to the size and scope of the establishment before hand. The "barriers to access" may be significant. When you do reach the appropriate person, the time that they will be willing to devote to your inquiry, will be short (e.g., remember how curt you may have been with the last telemarketer you spoke with).

Ask for the responsible manager or proprietor and introduce yourself. Inquire as to whether they are happy with their current cleaning service, what cleaning services they are currently receiving (i.e., type and frequency) and approximately what they are currently paying for their cleaning services.

Alternatively, you may wish to reference the name of your company, provided that you are prepared to follow up your inquiry with an invitation for an onsite consultation and you are "ready and able" to provide cleaning services to the business you are calling. The call then becomes a cold sales call, as well as a marketing research call.

Special interest bulletin boards and chat rooms are also useful forums, for finding out what individuals and businesses are paying for cleaning services. For instance, the NAPC website mentioned earlier, **www.cleanlink.com**, and other cleaning services related websites, have bulletin boards, on which you can ask members such questions.

Distributing customer surveys to targeted markets, has great value as a marketing research tool, because in addition to developing data about your potential customers' needs and price expectations, they can be combined with a brief introduction to your company and the services that you provide. Here again, offering special introductory rates or pricing, can provide an incentive for the recipient to respond.

Effective strategies for advertising and promoting your business

There are many forms of advertising and promotion, that small businesses can use, to help introduce their businesses into the market place.

- *Flyers*
- *Door hangers*
- *Postcards*
- *Customer surveys*
- *Neighborhood value pack mailers*
- *Business cards*
- *Classified ads in newspapers and magazines*
- *Brochures*
- *Yellow pages (telephone & internet)*
- *Internet websites and classified ads*
- *E-mail*
- *Registration with industry and community associations and commercial business listing services*

- *Press releases*
- *Radio ads*
- *Promotional CD's, video & audio and Cassettes*
- *Local or cable television ads*
- *Cold call & door to door sales*
- *Outdoor signs*
- *Mobile & removable signs*
- *Air balloon ads*

It is a very good idea, to examine the way other cleaning services are using each advertising medium, that you are planning to use, prior to spending or committing any of your valuable start-up capital. Then you should research the cost and features of each medium that you intend to use.

In each ad that you create, you should strive to include the standard components of effective cleaning services advertising, wherever possible.

Components of effective cleaning services advertising

- *an introduction that draws the attention of the viewer or listener*

- *an adequate description of your services*
- *industry experience, industry affiliations*
- *bonding & insurance information*
- *service areas*
- *contact information*
- *links to other forms of advertising that you are using currently using*

An in depth discussion of all of the forms of advertising listed above, is outside the scope of this book. However, you should continually search for innovative ways to advertise and promote your business, during its start-up and thereafter, as you work to expand your business. We will discuss some of the more basic and accessible forms of advertising here, as well as some more creative, or less traveled advertising media, that may be useful to your business in the future.

Print advertising media

An example of a flyer, for use in a targeted residential cleaning service promotion, was discussed earlier in this chapter. Other forms of print advertising that are effective, inexpensive and readily accessible, are:

- *door hangers;*
- *post cards;*
- *neighborhood value pack mailers;*
- *business cards;*
- *classified ads in newspapers;*
- *brochures.*

Door hangers are useful both as an introductory advertising tool, in order to introduce prospective customers to your business and as a promotional tool, to thank customers for using your service and to stimulate new, or repeat business.

Using a PC, a printer, paper and a scissors or Xacto knife, you can make door hangers for as little as 2 cents a piece (e.g., 3 per page, using a landscape printing format). Print advertising services and some creative resume services, will also prepare door hanger templates for a fee and provide cost effective copies, as well.

An example of a door hanger, used as a means of introducing a janitorial cleaning service to potential customers, is shown here. Door hangers are also convenient for advertising residential cleaning businesses, as well.

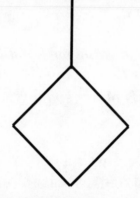

DISSATISFIED WITH YOUR CURRENT CLEANING SERVICE?

**CALL ACME JANITORIAL, Inc.
FOR A FREE
ONSITE CONSULTATION**

Phone: XXX-XXX-XXXX

We offer ...

- Competitive pricing
- High quality, reliable service
- Professional floor care services
- Fully bonded and insured employees
- More than 10 years professional
  experience

Use this door hanger
as a coupon for ...

(Over Please)

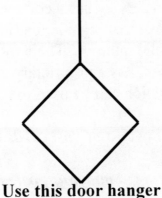

Use this door hanger as a coupon for:

- **20% off your next hard floor strip & wax.**

- **20% off your next carpet cleaning.**

See our ad in the yellow pages
or
Visit our website at
www.acme-janitorial.com

ACME JANITORIAL, Inc.
Owner/ operator: your name
Phone: XXX-XXX-XXXX
Mobile/ pager: XXX-XXX-XXXX
E-mail: e-mail@acme-janitorial.com

NAPC Member
(National Association of
Professional Cleaners)

The US postal service has a convenient and cost effective way of making and distributing **post cards,** all on the internet. Their website, **www.usps.com**, has a proprietary service called Net Post™, which can be used to:

- *calculate the cost of post cards and postage on-line;*
- *prepare and submit your post card text online;*
- *upload mailing lists on-line and automatically prepare post cards;*
- *mail post cards automatically, to potential customers, on-line, directly from the U.S. postal service.*

100 post cards (4.25" X 6"), can be prepared and mailed automatically, at a cost of $3.97 for the post cards and $17.40 for postage, for a total of $21.37 (2001 postal rates). There are many print advertising companies that also specialize in this type of advertising, which can be found in the yellow pages and on the internet.

You can generate your own mailing lists or purchase them from reputable direct mail marketers. Typical costs for mailing lists start at ~$25 per

1000 addresses or leads, sent to you in an electronic, CD or floppy disk file. These files can be uploaded to a PC and then cut and pasted for envelope or post card address printing, or they may be uploaded to an internet service such as Net Post™, that will do this for you. Many services will also provide preprinted adhesive address labels with their lists at no extra charge.

Direct mailing list data bases, are available on the internet and through other sources. They can be purchased, or in some cases, can be accessed for free from public records.

These lists can be very useful in identifying targeted groups of potential customers by various demographics, such as geographical area, income (i.e., for residential customers), business type etc.,. They can save a great deal of labor and time in preparing mailers, depending on the form (e.g., electronic files). Some of the categories that are available and may be useful, are new homeowners, affluent people (yes, such lists exist), professionals (e.g., doctors, lawyers etc.,), business organizations, government agencies, special interest groups and so on.

To ensure for the most effective and targeted direct mailing campaign, using public access or commercially acquired mailing lists, it may be helpful or important to:

- *find out how the lists were generated;*
- *find out how __current__, the list is;*
- *find out the form or medium, the list will distributed in and how you will __transfer__ addressee information to post cards, envelopes, e-mail letters etc.;*
- *specify addressee information, __only__ from the zip codes in which you provide services;*
- *determine the complete costs for direct mailing campaigns, including lists, mailing materials, postage, etc.,.*

Customer surveys, are another valuable tool to gather information about the needs of customers in your target markets, as well as what they are currently paying for their cleaning services. Customer surveys can be distributed in a variety of media such as flyers, post cards, value mailers, e-mail etc.,. Also, they can be coupled easily, to an introduction about your company's services and an invitation to prospective customers, to find out more about how your cleaning services can meet their needs.

To provide an <u>incentive</u> for the recipient to respond, you should consider including return
postage, offer a free gift, or include a discount
for future services etc., with your survey. An example of a customer survey on a post card, with
a company introduction and an offer for discounts on future services, is provided here.

ACME JANITORIAL Inc.,
Phone: xxx-xxx-xxxx, e-mail@acme-janitorial.com

Detach along perforated line

- -

Are you currently satisfied with your current cleaning service?
If not, we'd like introduce ourselves and invite you to answer a few
simple questions about your cleaning service needs. Return our
survey, or e-mail to us, a list of your current cleaning needs and the
rates that you are currently paying, to receive a **free** onsite consultation and initial cleaning, when you choose our service.

We offer...

- **Reliable, professional and courteous service**
- **Basic and specialized cleaning services, including profes-
sional floor care**
- **Fully bonded & insured employees** (insured by SZERLIP & CO., .)
- **Over 10 years experience**   **(over please)**

Return postage here

Return to: **Acme Janitorial**
xxxx Street, Anytown, Anystate, zip: xxxxx

What are you currently paying for services? $ _____
How many workers does your company have? _____
How long have you been using your present service? _____ yrs
What is the approximate size of your facility? _____ (sq. ft.)
How many times is your facility cleaned each week? _____
How many bathrooms does your facility have? _____
Does your facility require carpet care such as extraction cleaning, or hard
floor care, such as stripping and waxing ? _____
If so, what is approximate area of these floors? C_____ HF_____
Your facility's cleaning services contact: _____
Contact phone: _____ Alternate phone: _____
We look forward to serving your cleanings services needs soon!
See our ad in the **yellow pages**, or
Visit our website (**www.acme-janitorial.com**)

Neighborhood value mailers, such as **Val-Pak®**, send mailers to consumers, containing valuable coupons from local businesses providing good and services. They are located all over the United States and reach on average 10,000 consumers per mailing. The price for a single monthly mailing starts at ~$380. Their website address is (www.valpak.com).

The form of the mailer, is usually a single sheet approximately the size of a business envelope. There is ample space to introduce your cleaning service and provide information on prices and specials, as well as coupons and contact information. These mailers are ideal for residential cleaning services, or combined residential and commercial cleaning services.

Business cards, are usually not thought of as an advertising medium. However, simply leaving a card with a prospect, or their receptionist, on the windshield of their car, or in the door jam of their business or home, provides them with a brief introduction to your services and contact information, for future reference.

For example, if you have a website, the recipient

can log on to your website at a later date, for a fuller introduction to your services and view advertisements for specials. You should have business cards available with you at all times, when you are working, or in casual situations, where networking, or a chance meeting with someone in need of your services, is a possibility.

Classified ads are also a useful advertising tool. There are many community newspapers, that will charge a fee of $75, or less, to place ads, four weeks at a time. Many of these newspapers are free and have wide circulation. Many community newspapers also have websites and often, allow businesses to post ads in the newspaper and on-line simultaneously, at no extra charge. Classified ads, in community special interest or business trade magazines, may also allow you to target affluent residential customers, or select types of businesses.

Brochures can be considered an extension of the flyer as an advertising medium. They usually take the form of one or more folded or stapled sheets, or a short booklet. Brochures can provide detailed information about your company and its scope of services. They are often distributed to receptive customers during onsite consultations and they may be used as a visual aid during onsite presentations.

Advertising in your local phone company's **yellow pages**, can be a very important part of marketing your business. There may also be other "yellow pages", or commercial business listings in your city or town, that are effective ways of advertising and may be available to you, as well.

The yellow pages, are frequently used by persons and businesses that are new to the area or town where you live, in order to find their initial goods and services. It is possible to generate a sizeable amount of business with these new arrivals, using small ads as well as large ones.

Typically, prospective customers will be attracted to large ads initially, but may very well choose to call a business that is only listed by name, address and phone number, simply due to the fact that it is closer to where they live or work. Having said this, larger ads are often perceived as a sign of credibility, i.e., "... they have a large color ad ... they must be successful, reliable and trustworthy, etc.", are common thoughts that may come to mind, when people browse through the yellow pages for services.

Prices for ads in the yellow pages, range greatly, depending on the market you live in, as well as the features used in the ad, such as size, graphics, colors versus black or white, etc.,. Prices may range from a few hundred dollars per year, to several thousand dollars per year, for a full page color ad, in a large metropolitan area.

It is important in planning your advertising strategy, to be aware of the <u>cut-off date</u>, for submitting your ad, to the company preparing the yellow pages that you wish to advertise in, as they are often prepared only once a year. You may have to wait up to a year in order to have your ad listed, depending on the timing of your ad submission.

The cost of maintaining a separate business telephone account, is something to consider, in deciding to advertise in the yellow pages (or in any medium for that matter). You should factor into your "yellow pages advertising budget", a minimum of ~$45/month for an additional phone line, depending on the area that you live in.

An additional phone line will separate your business and personal phone traffic, and lend credibility to your business. An inexpensive alternative, is the use of a virtual voice mail service. In this instance, a virtual phone number with voicemail capability is charged to your existing home phone for ~$15/month.

The internet and related advertising media

A full discussion of the vast number of ways in which you can advertise on the internet is outside the scope of this guide. For a full treatment of free, or inexpensive ways to advertise on the internet, surf the internet, or purchase one of many excellent books on the subject. A few of the most basic, cost effective and readily accessible methods, will be discussed here.

Websites are becoming an increasingly important advertising tool to many businesses, including small businesses, such as a cleaning service start-up. They are useful in many respects, but perhaps some of the most important reasons that they are useful for a small business, are:

- *websites allow you to __expand__ an introduc-*

tion to your business and the description of its products and services, including discounts and specials, well beyond most print advertising media, through the use of 2 or more linked web pages (websites are typically 1-5 pages, for this type of application);

- *many business and increasingly, individual consumers, are using the internet as an effective alternative or supplement to the local telephone yellow pages, when <u>searching</u> for goods and services. Finding information about a cleaning service, can be as easy as <u>typing key words</u> such as "cleaning services" and the "name" of the city in which they work or live, into a <u>search engine</u> and then clicking a highlighted <u>hypertext link</u>, in the results list that appears on the screen;*

- *having a website can be an effective tie-in or link to other forms of advertising that your business may be using, as well as extending <u>credibility</u> to your business and its image.*

- *customers can make <u>inquiries</u>, to describe their cleaning service needs and name a price or fee they are willing to pay, by com-*

municating with your business directly, through e-mail links provided on your website *(and you should invite them to do so, by specifying the reasons that they might wish to e-mail your business).*

Most cleaning services businesses incorporate into their websites, the same components for effective cleaning services advertising, that were discussed in conjunction with flyers. An example of a **home page** for a cleaning services website, is presented here. The layout and process of designing a website, for either a home cleaning business or janitorial service, is nearly identical.

As you can see in the example, a business can accomplish a great deal with the home page of its website, in the way of providing details about its products and services and towards inviting responses from prospective customers. A website that provides e-mail links, extends a means by which the viewer can immediately contact your business with information about their cleaning needs. Such information, can help you determine the scope of the customer's cleaning needs and a establish a clever starting point for you to make a competitive bid for their services. Many internet services such as **Yahoo!**, provide web page hosting and web page building services for <u>free</u> (i.e., Yahoo! Geocities), that may be an ideal solution, provided that you or some one that you know, can follow pop up menus and perform straight forward "click and drag" functions, to insert objects, texts, link addresses into a blank web page(s).

This much, will allow you to reference your website in other forms of advertising, thereby allowing a prospective customer to type your web address into their internet browser and reach your website. It will <u>not</u> make your website accessible in random or general searches, using a search window or box, connected with existing internet directories or search engines.

For this type of exposure, you will need to "**prepare**" your web pages using "**meta tags**" for <u>titles</u>, <u>keywords</u> and <u>descriptions</u>, that are inserted into the HTML code of your web pages and allow search engines to detect and index your website. You then "**submit**" your website for registration or listing with various search engines.

There is an art and a skill, to being placed at, or near the top of the list of responses to a search engine query. **Preparation** and **submission** of your website to search engines, may also be done for <u>free</u> using internet services such as **Ya-hoo!**, but involves acquired skills, that are usually beyond the current skill sets of most individuals. Depending on various factors, such as the particular search engine involved and the method of your submission, it can take up to 6 months from the time of submission to a search engine, until your website is "turning up" in responses to website queries.

Many internet services provide these types of services, as part of fee based packages that include, for example:

- *domain name registration;*
- *website hosting;*
- *website designing services or access to web site design software;*
- *preparation and submission to search engines.*

Some of these internet services cost substantially less than $50/month, with varying degrees of success in getting your website registered or listed with major search engines. However, not all of these website development companies will provide search engine preparation and submission services. Many local chambers of commerce chapters, also sponsor some type of web hosting, or internet listing services, for small businesses, that may be worth investigating.

Other useful internet related forms of advertising, including e-mail advertising, registration with business listing services, linking to other websites, networking through chat rooms etc., are outside the scope of this guide and are left for the reader to explore.

ACME JANITORIAL SERVICE, Inc.

Acme Cleaning Service, Inc.
Servicing: Anytown, USA
Owner: Your Name
Phone: xxx-xxx-xxxx
Cellular/pager: xxx-xxx-xxxx
Fully Bonded & Insured by: SZERLIP & CO., Inc

Serving the greater "Any Town USA" area since 1995

We are proud members of the NAPC (National association of professional cleaners) and the IICRC
(Institute for Inspection, Cleaning and Restoration)

Our courteous staff of cleaning technicians are fully bonded and insured. We offer reliable, professional basic cleaning services, as well as a range of special services, such as deep cleaning, hard floor care, carpet care and exterior pressure washing.

We invite you to call us about our rates and the services that we provide, or

send us an e-mail:
- detailing your cleaning needs; or
- to provide us with a quote, for what you are currently paying for cleaning services, in order to see if we can save you money; or
- to set-up an appointment for a free consultation

Underlined portions of text are hyper-text links to additional web pages, or the web site's e-mail address

Home page Basic Cleaning Services Carpet Care Hard Floor Care
Pressure Washing Deep Cleaning Areas of service Coupons & Discounts What to include in your list of cleaning needs FAQ
Contact Us

Other forms of advertising

Other forms of advertising that can be effective and may be accessible to the small cleaning service start-up, are radio and cable television advertising, outdoor signs and signs/ lettering on your vehicle.

Floor and upholstery care services advertise occasionally on **local radio** and **television**. Cleaning services use these advertising mediums less frequently. Having said this, both radio and television can be useful advertising media for a cleaning services business that serves <u>residential</u> customers, if they are used at <u>appropriate</u> stages in the development or expansion of a business, and provided that they are properly used and monitored.

Radio can also useful for cleaning services that serve small businesses. Talk radio for instance, is an extremely popular advertising medium for advertising all types of service based businesses, ranging from heating and air conditioning to cleaning services.

The price of a single 60 second radio commercial, can range from less than $100 per spot, to as much as $1800 or more, depending on a variety of factors, such as:

- *the size of the listening market;*
- *the time of day the ad runs;*
- *seasonal rates that may apply;*
- *production costs and radio personality endorsement fees.*

A good idea to consider, in trying to reach significant groups of listeners cheaply, is to advertise on small stations, such as religious broadcasting stations, on Sunday mornings, for instance. A pitch, such as "mention this radio commercial and receive a 20% discount ...", can help to attract customers and will allow you to track the effectiveness of your advertising.

Another useful strategy for stretching your radio or television advertising dollars, is to run ads during holidays, when people are more likely to be watching or listening. It goes without saying, that the best time to run radio ads is during morning and afternoon rush hours. These are prime advertising hours, but advertising during these time slots will increase the cost of your ads, accordingly.

Local cable television advertising may also be a useful medium to try, as well. Ads can run as low as $250-$275 for a 30 second spot on cable television in some markets, with production costs that run as low as $375-$875.

During your initial start-up, you should consider concentrating on the more traditional and basic advertising media that are used by most cleaning services, such as print and internet related advertising. As your resources grow and you understand your markets better, you may wish to experiment with broadcasting media, as well.

For example, referencing a broadcast ad that you are running during the holidays, concurrently in your print or internet advertising, may help to distinguish your business from your competitors, in the eyes of a prospective client and secure an inquiry leading to an onsite consultation.

Radio and television advertising sales departments can also provide you with pricing and advertising strategies. However, keep in mind at all times, that their primary job is to generate the highest advertising sales possible, for their station.

Vanity license plates, license plate frames and vehicle signs/ lettering are effective mobile forms of advertising. They are inexpensive and are always working for you, when your vehicle is on the road, or when it can be viewed by passers by in public places.

A **license plate** with "JANITOR", "CLEANER" or "WECLNIT", for example, surrounded by a plate frame with your company's name and phone number, can be a very effective and passive form of advertising to try. Placing **Signs and lettering** on your vehicle is equally effective, costing as little as ~$30, in some cases.

"Cold calling", "door to door" solicitation and **networking**, are advertising staples that you should consider as part of your advertising strategy, at some point. "Blanketing" a target market or area with flyers or door hangers, before you make cold sales calls, or onsite solicitations, can provide potential customers, some advance awareness of your company and its services. You can then call or greet residential and busi-

nesses customers personally, making reference
to your flyer or door hanger as a "lead in" to
your solicitation.

When networking or conducting door to door
solicitations, always leave a flyer or business
card with <u>receptive</u> prospects. They will need
some means, that provides them with the information they need to contact you at a later date,
in order to set an appointment, or to obtain more
information about your services and pricing.

People tend to be more receptive to doing business with people that they have met in person
and feel comfortable with. However, when soliciting in person, be advised that many businesses, apartment complexes and living communities have policies prohibiting solicitation. Ig-
noring these policies may be viewed as an inva-
sion of privacy and could subject you to prosecution, should you persist.

Fear of rejection, shyness, or poor articulation
are often "barriers to success", in person to person exchanges or dialogues. Some common
sense fundamentals of business interaction are
provided here, to help provide focus and direc-

tion in this area. These are the same fundamentals that you would employ in an interview with a prospective employer. In a sense, that's exactly what you are doing in a sales call or meeting, "going on an interview", in order to convince the client to "offer you a job".

Fundamentals of business interaction

- *Always be <u>well groomed</u> and <u>dress neatly</u> when representing your company in solicitations and during business meetings*

- *Greet prospective customers with <u>direct</u> eye contact, a genuine smile and a firm handshake (a handshake can be considered forward and may not always appropriate in a "door to door" solicitation)*

- *Speak politely, articulately and confidently, with a <u>purpose</u> in mind, in order to convey information about your business, find out about the customer's needs, set appointments, or when negotiating prices and services (working from scripts that you have prepared and rehearsed in advance, can be very helpful in many situations, such as an* *initial greeting on the telephone, during on-site presentations of your services, etc., until you have developed a confident and effective style)*

- **Avoid <u>negative</u> lines of reasoning, or criticism of competitors**

- **Be brief, but not curt and always thank the prospective customer, for sharing a part of his or her valuable time**

Regardless of the type of advertising strategies that you use:

- **be <u>realistic</u> in your expectations, for attracting or securing business through any advertising strategy that you use;**

- **continually monitor the cost and effectiveness of your advertising, by soliciting feedback and by <u>recording</u> how clients found out about your services;**

- **periodically <u>refine</u> your advertising techniques in order to remain contemporary and to enhance their effectiveness.**

Chapter 5

Determining a price for your services:

In this chapter, we will discuss some of the critical factors and processes that are involved in determining a price for your services, preparing and submitting business proposals and negotiating with clients. Topics that will be a part of our discussion, are:

- *factors involved in preparing a bid estimate or price structure;*

- *bidding formulas and cost of service calculations;*

- *determining production rates and the process of work loading;*

- *bidding requirements and cleaning specifications;*

- *preparing and submitting your bid proposal;*

- *negotiating with clients.*

Factors involved in preparing a bid estimate or price structure

There are a variety of approaches and techniques for estimating the total cost of a service provided to a client. These approaches and techniques are applicable to a host of service based industries, such as:

- *general, electrical, plumbing, HVAC, sheet rock, roofing, and flooring contractors;*

- *IT, webmaster and software consultants;*

- *"job shops", such as cabinet makers, metal fabricators, print shops, etc.;*

- *landscaping, janitorial, institutional house-keeping and floor care service contractors;*

and so on.

All of these businesses prepare bid proposals, or price structures, using detailed estimates for basic factors associated with providing goods and services competitively, while still maintaining a reasonable profit. The same basic process is used by virtually all businesses, to establish standard pricing structures, for the goods and services that we use everyday, in our personal lives.

These basic factors are:

- **overhead costs**
  (e.g., building leases, utilities, transportation, licenses, business insurance, bonding, employee insurance, capital equipment such as floor care equipment, offices supplies, advertising, etc.,);

- **labor**
  (direct labor costs, payroll taxes, independent contractors, subcontractors, consultants, supervision, management, etc.,);

- **materials and supplies**
  (e.g., cleaning solutions, floor finishes, strippers, carpet extraction solutions, mop heads, small cleaning tools, as well as the cost of supplies resold to customers);

- *profit margin*

Bidding formulas and
cost of service calculations

An idealized example, using basic math, may be helpful to illustrate how these basic factors are used to determine a rate or price for services.

For example, an aspiring entrepreneur has a solo janitorial service. He works out of his home and owns a floor machine and a carpet extractor. At present, he has four <u>identical</u> accounts. Our contractor has purchased his equipment, supplies and advertising, on credit and is making monthly payments on these items. Additionally, he has determined that his labor is worth a minimum of $10.50/ hr and he is charging each of his accounts $600/ month, based on advice given to him by an experienced contractor.

The contractor said that as a rule of thumb, our entrepreneur should consider charging a rate that will yield a minimum of 30% after labor*, that is:

$$(\$600-\$420/ \text{ mo}) \div \$600 = \$180 \text{ and}$$

$$(\$180/ \$600) * 100 = 30\%$$

* bidding formulas, using fixed percentages to determine a profit margin, after overhead and account related costs, are common in many service industries. Some cleaning industry professionals recommend 30%, as a reasonable profit margin for cleaning services start-ups to consider charging, in instances where the market will bear it. Profit margins will generally be lower for larger accounts, particularly in cases where a competitive bidding process is employed. Knowing the current price that a prospective client is paying, along with your total costs, will allow you to determine the range of profit margin that is appropriate.

He is currently negotiating with a prospective client, that has cleaning services needs, identical to those of his four existing accounts. The prospective client has rejected the verbal offer that was made by our entrepreneur, during the initial onsite consultation, which is the same rate that he currently charges his four existing accounts. The customer has asked him to provide a lower rate in his written bid proposal.

To summarize, in order for our contractor to determine the lowest price that he can bid on a 5th identical account and adhere to the following criteria:

- *maintain the same labor rate for his time;*

COMMERCIAL & RESIDENTIAL CLEANING SERVICES

- *pay off his equipment and supplies at the same monthly rate;* and

- *spread his overhead costs, <u>evenly</u>, across all 5 accounts;*

the following approach might be used.

Current finances for 4 existing accounts:

Over head:
- Business license ... $96/ 12 mo= $ 8/ mo
- liability insurance .... $ 75/ mo
- Fidelity bond ... $120/ 12 mo= $ 10/ mo
- Floor machine ... $660/ 12 mo= $ 55/ mo
- Carpet extractor ... $660/ 12 mo= $ 55/ mo
  (demonstrator model)
- Janitor's cart ... $132/ 12 mo= $ 11/ mo
- Bucket & wringer ...$108/ 12 mo= $ 9/ mo
- Amortized rent & utilities
  (works out of his home, appropriate deductions taken at the end of the year)
- Mobile phone ... $ 35/ mo
- Virtual voice mail ... $ 15/ mo

- Website ... $ 25/ mo
- Transportation ...$0. 345x446 mi= $154/ mo
- Billing supplies ... $24/ 12 mo= $ 2/ mo
- 100 Business cards, 500 flyers ... $ 50/ mo
                                    total $504/ mo

Materials and supplies: (for 4 accounts)
- Mops, brooms ... $48/ 12 mo= $ 4/   mo
- scrub/buff pads ...$336/ 12 mo= $ 28/   mo
- Carpet cleaners ... $156/ 12 mo= $ 13/   mo
- Cleaners ... $132/ 12 mo= $ 11/   mo
- Stripper & wax ... $1600/12 mo=$ 133/ mo
- Trash liners ... $ 12/ mo
- Uniform shirts ...5 x $40/12 mo $ 16/   mo
                                    total $216/   mo

Labor:
- Acct 1... ((1.75 hr x 20 d)+5 hr/mo*) x $10.5= $420/ mo
- Acct 2... ((1.75 hr x 20 d)+5 hr/mo*) x $10.5= $420/ mo
- Acct 3... ((1.75 hr x 20 d)+5 hr/mo*) x $10.5= $420/ mo
- Acct 4... ((1.75 hr x 20 d)+5 hr/mo*) x $10.5= $420/ mo
                                    total $1680/ mo

Gross Sales
- Acct 1 ... (1.43 x $420/mo)= $600/ mo
- Acct 2 ... (1.43 x $420/mo)= $600/ mo
- Acct 3 ... (1.43 x $420/mo)= $600/ mo
- Acct 4 ... (1.43 x $420/mo)= $600/ mo
                                    total $2400/ mo

Gross profit before taxes:

($2400 — $720) = $1680/ mo
(70% of gross sales**)

*Note: the work loading in this example reflects routine cleaning five days/ week, with 5 hrs/mo floor care charged at the same labor rate, in order to complete quarterly floor care. In practice, floor care is often quoted separately from general cleaning. Rates charged to businesses for floor care are typically higher than those charged for general cleaning. This example is simplified, for the purpose of illustrating the general principles of bid estimating.

For simplicity, the overhead remains fixed and the increased cost of materials and supplies in going from 4 to 5 accounts, is estimated with a simple ratio (i.e., (5 ÷ 4) x $216 = $270), even though there are no new expenses for mops/ brooms and uniforms, etc.,.

So, in order to determine the minimum bid for the 5th account under these conditions, we could make the following simple calculations:

($504 + $270) ÷   5   = $155/account
total (overhead + materials)   ÷ (total no. accounts) = (overhead + materials)/ account

and

($420   + $155   )   = $575/ mo
   (labor)   (overhead + material)   (new bid price)

$575/ mo is the new bid price for the 5th account. Gross sales and gross profit with the 5th account, are:

Gross Sales:
- Acct 1 ... (1.43 x $420/mo)= $600/ mo
- Acct 2 ... (1.43 x $420/mo)= $600/ mo
- Acct 3 ... (1.43 x $420/mo)= $600/ mo
- Acct 4 ... (1.43 x $420/mo)= $600/ mo
- Acct 5 ... (1.37 x $420/mo)= $575/ mo
                 total= $2975/ mo

Gross profit before taxes:
($2975   — $773)   = $2202/ mo
                              (74% of gross sales**)

Our hard working entrepreneur is now <u>committed</u> to a total of 8.75 hrs daily, to clean all 5 accounts and ~6.25 hrs, each weekend for floor care, not including travel time. Still, he feels up to cleaning a 6th account, as all of the businesses are in close proximity to each other. Also, he has reduced the <u>actual</u> cleaning time per account, by 0.25 hr per day, through sheer repetition and thoughtful efficiency.

A 2nd prospective client knows the owner of the 5th account, and is a competitor, who will switch services, only if he receives a small discount over his business rival.

Using the same approach, the lowest bid on the 6th account is:

($420   + $138)   = $558/ mo,
  (labor)   (overhead, materials, labor)   (new bid prices)

the gross sales = $3533/ mo; and

gross profit before taxes= $2705/ mo,
                    (~76% of gross sales**)

Or $32,460/ year (before tax deductions taken at the end of the year)

Note that his equipment will be paid for in one year. If he makes no changes in his business, in his second year, he will make $34,020 before tax deductions.

**For the purposes of our example, "labor" is calculated as if our entrepreneur is paying himself for the labor he performs. However, the values for his "gross profit before taxes" in this example include the "cost" of his personal labor as profit (i.e., similar to wages before taxes). Please note that costs due to wages paid to <u>others</u> for labor, would subtracted from his gross sales, along with overhead and materials, in order to determine his gross profit before taxes.

Going forward, our entrepreneur will very likely have to change his strategy in order to expand his business. For example, he could hire a part time employee, or an independent contractor, to work one or more of his accounts, so that he can devote more time to sales, recruitment of personnel, etc.,.

It should also be noted, that he will see a reduction in his overhead, once his equipment is completely paid for. He can reduce his costs for overhead and supplies further, by shopping vigilantly for cheaper supplies and services.

Our example, although idealized and tailored to a solo janitorial services start-up, provides an illustration of how the basic factors involved in the bid estimating process may be used to establish a competitive bid price. In this example, there are no considerations for taking year end deductions for business expenses, or paying income taxes and self employment taxes.

As a self employed individual, you will need to quantify these additional factors, in order to determine what your estimated <u>net</u> income will be, month to month. For this, you should strongly consider consulting a lawyer, accountant, or tax service, unless you have prepared taxes for a self employed person in the past, or until you have learned with confidence, how to prepare them yourself.

In most cases, you will have to establish the discipline for saving, or escrowing monthly, 1/12th of your annual estimated self employment and income taxes, in order to avoid owing taxes at the end of the year. Those who are self employed in a trade or a profession, generally have to report their net earnings over $400, to social security, in a schedule SE form, unless they are eligible for an alternate approach.

Our example shows a basic approach for distributing the cost of your overhead, across all of your accounts. Adding this incremental overhead cost, to the cost of materials, supplies and labor, needed to service a single new account, establishes a basis or breakeven point for that account. After that, how you determine your bidding price, profit margin, or gross profit before taxes, is a mix of:

- *what the market will bear at any given point in time, right down to the individual client;*

- *what you must earn to sustain the business and make progress towards reaching your financial goals.*

Experienced small business entrepreneurs and

**Simple bidding formula
for a bidding estimate breakeven point**
(i.e., cost basis before profit margin)

(total overhead ÷ total number of accounts) +

(materials & supplies per account) =

breakeven point per account

---

business managers, whether they are in construction contracting, custom fabrication or installation, consulting groups, or other services, have all learned how to bid, through practice, knowledge of their particular markets and by careful quantification, using the basic bid estimating factors presented earlier. It should be mentioned that there are more sophisticated methods for distributing overhead than shown in the preceding example, such as the use of weighted distributions.

For example, say that you have one account that comprises 80% of your business and a second client that accounts for the remaining 20%. You wish to add a third account, identical to the smaller of your first two accounts. To redistribute your overhead across all three accounts, you would add up the overhead costs for all three accounts first.

Then you would make a rough estimate of the percentage of gross sales, that all three accounts contribute, making a <u>pre-bid</u> assumption that the 3rd account's gross sales will equal that of the 2nd account. Finally, you would redistribute your overhead costs across each account, according to their relative contribution in sales. In this case, 60% of the total overhead is assigned to the largest account, and 20% to each of the 2 smaller accounts, for a total of 100%.

A similar way to distribute overhead costs across all of your accounts, is to figure the overhead for any single account, as a percentage of the total cost of materials, supplies and labor for all of your accounts.

This approach eliminates the need for a "pre-bid

**Distribution of overhead
based on a percentage of
materials, supplies & labor**

<u>(materials, supplies, labor for each account)</u> x 100 x
(<u>total</u> costs for all materials, supplies & labor)

(total overhead) = (% overhead per account)

---

gross sales" assumption, for a new account (i.e., approximate gross sales before the final bid) and potential skew, due to any significant variations in the profit margins for pre-existing accounts.

Determining production rates and the process of work loading

If you do not have prior cleaning services experience, a good place to start gaining insight and experience in estimating cleaning times, is to practice cleaning at home, at a friend's or relative's home or business, after a church function, following your apartment complex's clubhouse party etc.,. <u>Measure</u> the area of the each room you clean and <u>record</u> your cleaning times for each type of task, such as vacuuming, cleaning bathrooms etc.,.

Contemplate how you can apply, or "scale-up" your cleaning rates (i.e., cleaning time per area, or production rates), to estimate cleaning times for larger facilities. Observe the logistics for emptying trash, vacuuming etc., in the public places or businesses that you visit, as part of a bidding exercise, or training drill for an onsite consultation.

These exercises are excellent practice and rehearsal for your first walk through and onsite consultation. Another useful technique is to continue measuring and recording cleaning data, once you begin cleaning accounts, in order to expand and refine your estimates for cleaning times, for various cleaning tasks and facility types.

These cleaning times, when expressed as a rate per unit square area (e.g., building area, office area, bathroom area, lounge area, etc.,), are often referred to as <u>production rates</u> in the commercial cleaning industry. After a while, you may not be able to resist the temptation to "guesstimate", what you might charge to clean a building that you have entered for the first time. This type of mental exercise, will help to reduce your bid estimating learning curve, far more rapidly, than if you only concentrate your energies on each actual business prospect, that you encounter.

Practicing cleaning tasks and measuring and recording the data, in order to establish production rates, is similar to the Michael Jordan analogy mentioned in chapter one. Namely, how professional athletes use drills to improve their skills, such as running, jumping, throwing, shooting catching, etc., that are so essential to improving their performances. Analyzing films of yourself during "cleaning sprints", however, is most likely, over doing it!

For those unfamiliar with, or "rusty" at calculating the area of a room, or the area of cleaning spaces in a building, they are usually measured in square feet in the United States and in square meters, abroad. If you don't have a tape measure at hand yet, a quick way to estimate the area of a room, is to walk the room lengthwise, "toe to heel" and repeat, in the widthwise direction. Then assume 1 ft for each foot step (or ~0.31 m step) and multiply the number of lengthwise steps by the number of widthwise steps.

For example:

50 steps x 50 steps = ~2500 sq. ft.
or
50 steps x 50 steps = ~232 sq. m., (~240 with round off).

The Stanley® INTELLIMEASURE™, Laser ultrasonic estimator, or its equivalent, is a useful tool for gathering data in the estimation of production rates, or in calculating the usage of supplies for floor care work. Starting at ~$80, they are used widely in construction and serviced based businesses and are accurate to 5%, for a distance of 50 feet. Simply point the device at the floor, or adjacent walls and the display provides an estimate of square feet, or meters, for that area. It's a great work saver that can help you to expedite an onsite consultation quickly, give you confidence in your estimates and enhance your credibility with clients.

Consider generating a list or table of cleaning times for various cleaning tasks or operations, that you can use for bidding and employee allocation purposes (i.e., work loading). Include as a part of your list, specifications such as the rate per bathroom cleaning, window washing, or vacuuming and sweeping, as a rate per sq. ft., etc.,. This information, can then be used to scale up estimates of production rates for larger facilities, once you have the necessary cleaning area estimates.

For example, if you can clean a reasonably well maintained small bathroom at home, in say 10 minutes (i.e., to empty the trash, clean the toilet and sink fixtures, mop the floor and to refill the soap and toilet paper, as needed), then it is fairly easy task to estimate the total cleaning time for the bathrooms in a small business.

For instance, in a well maintained building, with four bathrooms that have 2 toilets and 2 sinks in each, you might estimate the total cleaning time for the bathrooms in the facility as follows:

10 min. per one toilet & sink combination, and the adjoining floor ÷ 60 min. = 0.167 hrs per bathroom "unit"

and

3 min. to move materials and supplies ÷ 60 = 0.05 hr between bathrooms

and

4 bathrooms x 2 toilet & sink combinations x 0.167 hr = 1.04 hrs

1.04 hrs + (4 x 0.05 hrs) = 1.54 hrs,

or

~ 1.5 hrs total cleaning time* and ~23 minutes per bathroom*

* the time necessary to stage equipment & supplies is not included here.

From there, you could calculate a production rate "of sorts" for cleaning bathrooms. To do this, divide the total floor area for all four bathrooms, by the total cleaning time estimated for all four bathrooms, to obtain a production rate expressed in square feet per hour. The drawback to the use of such a production rate estimate, is that it may not provide adequate accuracy for all work loading situations.

For example, what if there are 3 toilets, 3 urinals, 3 sinks per bathroom and the bathroom floor is 2.5 times larger, than in the last example? What if all the bathrooms in a facility are not uniform?

A more straight forward and accurate approach, that is used by many commercial cleaning professionals, is to calculate the cleaning time required for each specific task, or operation involved in cleaning a bathroom and then multiply the total number of each type of operation that is required in the facility, by the cleaning time or production rate for that type of operation. Then the products (i.e., the total no. of each operation x the cleaning time for that operation), are totaled for all operations.

Additionally, factors such as the frequency per week, or month, that each operation is performed and the number of employees that are used for each operation, may be included in such calculations, in order to get a total picture of the time and labor involved for each task or operation. Since we have already discussed estimating cleaning times for bathrooms, an example of work loading for bathrooms is presented here.

Bathroom work loading example
(5 bathrooms)

operation	total no. or area	clean time* (per person)	frequency (per month)	employees/ operation	total time (hours)
mop floors	1250 sq. ft.	0.25 hr/ 1000 sq. ft.	20	1	6.25
toilet	10	0.03 hrs (1.8 min)	20	1	6
urinal	6	0.03 hrs (1.8 min)	20	1	3.6
sink	10	0.03 hrs	20	1	6
mirror	10	0.03 hrs	20	1	6
soap	10	0.015 hrs (~1 min)	20	1	3
paper towels	5	0.015 hrs	20	1	1.5
tissue paper	10	0.015 hrs	20	1	3
sanitary napkin	2	0.015 hrs	20	1	0.6
Empty trash	10	0.015 hrs	20	1	3

total cleaning time per month	39 hrs
time per cleaning (i.e., per day)	1.95 hrs
cleaning time per bathroom	0.39 (23 min)

*cleaning times and production rates for this example, are idealized for the purpose of this illustration. Values may vary from those taken from published tables or those generated by the reader. Actual cleaning times will vary with the staging and cleaning techniques used, the equipment used, the amount of supply replacement required at each cleaning and the amount of soiling between cleaning intervals.

The process of determining the time and labor required for a group of cleaning tasks or operations, is formally referred to as **work loading** in the commercial cleaning industry. Work loading calculations are usually based on such data as building and customer cleaning specifications, cleaning time or production rate estimates, available labor, team cleaning concepts and cleaning frequency or work intervals (i.e., daily, weekly, monthly etc.,). With the addition of such data as distributed overhead, labor, materials and supply, cost estimates, a complete "cost of service" estimate can be generated, for any given facility or account.

In the case of a home cleaning business just starting out, the time it takes to clean your own home or apartment, serves as a good starting point for establishing cleaning times and production rates. From there, you can determine your rates or pricing structures, based on overhead costs, such as bonding, insurance, equipment and transportation, as well as the hourly rate that you feel you must charge, in order to make a profit and still remain competitive.

An example of one type of **pricing structure** for apartment cleaning, is provided here. The pricing structures for your services will vary, based on the market you are in and what you feel you must earn in exchange for the cost of your labor, insurance, equipment etc.,. This example is not applicable to a "turnkey" or "make ready" cleaning scenario, which may involve more extensive cleaning.

The home cleaning service in this price structure example, is charging a premium for a single monthly cleaning. The additional work involved in cleaning a month's accumulation of dirt and grime, coupled with the time and expense, that may be caused by a deviation from a set cleaning route, in order to reach a single customer, may be the rational behind the pricing here.

Basic cleaning includes: mopping; sweeping; vacuuming; cleaning bathroom fixtures; cleaning kitchen counter tops; emptying the trash, etc.,. Deep cleaning services may include upgrades, such as cleaning the outside of cabinets and appliances, behind furniture etc.,. Extras that may be added, are cleaning the interior of appliances such as refrigerators, dusting, etc., at prices ranging from $5-$25.

The prices for introductory cleaning, are being used here, as an incentive to attract customers and to allow them to see the quality of the work the service provides. An introductory cleaning is often agreed to by the customer, in advance of the onsite consultation, in order to recoup the time and expense for the sales call and to ensure earnest intent, on the part of the prospective customer.

Note also, that the pricing in this example may be intended to allow for convenient payment by the customer in paper denominations. This eliminates the need for customers to keep pocket change on hand, in order to pay the cleaning service in exact change and also avoids unnecessary handling of change by employees.

Home cleaning services may also structure their fees by charging a standard hourly rate. Some home cleaning professionals report hourly rates, ranging from approximately $12 to $25, or more. Still others, may perform an initial cleaning of a home or apartment, according to the customer's instructions, at a prearranged hourly rate, and then quote or negotiate a rate, or price structure with the customer, afterwards.

Similar approaches, are common to introductory offers made by many businesses, in other service industries. The use of introductory or initial cleaning offers, can be helpful to small janitorial services, that are soliciting new business from

Sample price structure for
apartment cleaning services

Apartment size	Basic	price	Deep	price
1 bed	weekly	$20	weekly	$25
1 bath	bi-weekly	$30	bi-weekly	$35
	monthly	$65	monthly	$75
2 & 3 bed	weekly	$25	weekly	$30
2 bath	bi-weekly	$35	bi-weekly	$40
	monthly	$85	monthly	$95
Initial clean	**Basic**	$15	**Deep**	$20

small and medium sized establishments.

The purpose of an introductory cleaning offer made by janitorial contractors, is the same as the initial cleaning offer shown in the apartment cleaning price structure example. However, the hourly rate that the contractor actually uses for an initial cleaning, is not usually disclosed in an advertisement and may not be determined, until the contractor inspects the facility, or learns what the client is currently paying for cleaning services.

NOA's, bidding requirements, and cleaning specifications

Federal, state and local governments, are required by law to make available to the public, **notice of awards** (**NOA**'s) and bidding requirements or specifications, for all of the contracts that they enter into, with companies in the private sector. This is in the interest of fair disclosure, so that companies in the private sector can bid fairly, on contracts to provide the types goods and services that are used by various government agencies, going forward.

NOA's and bidding requirements for janitorial

and housekeeping services contracts, are posted on the internet, or are available by fax or mail, through federal, state, county, or city purchasing agencies. You can also call the facility whose cleaning services contract you are interested in bidding on, directly, for posting information.

These documents become a matter of public record when they are posted and they often provide a wealth of detailed information about:

- ***cleaning contract specifications***
  (e.g., cleaning frequencies, cleaning requirements or protocols, such as wet mopping floors, dusting surfaces, vacuuming, sweeping etc.,);

- ***building specifications***
  (total building square footage, floor type and square footage, number of employees, amount of public traffic, number of bathrooms, number of bathroom fixtures);

- ***contractor and employee specifications***
  (supervisory experience, employee qualifications);
- ***pricing structures***

(e.g., monthly and annual rates in dollars per square feet, total monthly fees, emergency cleaning rates, etc.,);

- **terms and conditions**
  (e.g., bidding submission requirements, performance based incentives, contract renewal and cancellation, payment, etc.,);

- **successful bid prices**
  (actual winning bid prices, top 3 bid prices etc.,).

Key phrases, such as "janitorial services contract notice of award", "janitorial services contract specifications", etc., may be helpful when searching on-line for this type of information. **www.pagevendor.com**, has convenient links to various state web pages. From there, look for purchasing and then look for janitorial service contracts, specifications and notice of awards, etc.,.

If your state is not listed there, try using an internet search string that contains the name of your state, county, or city and the words "government" or "purchasing". Most states will

have some type of internet access to their purchasing agency.

A simplified example of the type of information
available in NOA postings and bidding specifications, is shown here (i.e., requirements are
simulated and actual award data is not repro-
duced here). Studying examples of pertinent
NOA's, or bidding specifications, that contain
cleaning specifications and service agreement
terms, such as those shown here, will help you
immensely in the preparation of your bid proposals for government contracts.

Compliance with the bidding specifications of
government agencies, is almost always a prereq-
uisite for a successful bid. Failure to meet any
of the terms and conditions for submitting a bid,
could invalidate your bid.

These documents can also be used selectively, as
templates for establishing the components of bid
proposals and standard service agreements or
contracts, that your company uses in soliciting
business in the private sector, as well.

The sample (NOA/ cleaning specification/ clean-

Sample Notice of Award
for a janitorial services contract
(with service agreement specifications)

Building specifications:
Total cleanable square feet: 24,000 sq. ft.
- Carpeted area: 22,000 sq. ft.
- Vinyl area: 500 sq. ft.
- Restroom area: ceramic tile, 1,500 sq. ft.

Restrooms: total 6; 3 male, 3 female
- Sinks: 12
- Urinals: 3
- Toilets: 12

Windows: 120

Cleaning specifications:
Cleaning hours:
- All work to be done between the hours of 5PM and 6AM the following morning

Maximum cleaning rate:
- 2500 sq. ft. per person per hour (maximum production rate per person allowed)

Daily:
- Dust all of the following surfaces with chemically treated dust cloth or mop: stairwells, floors, chairs, cabinets, tables, pictures, fire extinguishers ...)
- Sweep or mop all hard floor surfaces
- Vacuum all carpeted surfaces
- Empty all trash receptacles daily and remove to dumpsters
- Empty or consolidate all recyclables (m, w, f)
- Clean and sanitize bathroom fixtures, drinking fountains as needed

Weekly:
- Damp mop stairwells
- Buff hard flooring

167

- Wash bathroom fixtures and floors
- Spray wax and buff ceramic tile with wax, that has a non-slide formulation

Monthly:
- Remove all smudge marks from applicable surfaces such as door casings, floor moldings or skirts

Quarterly:
- Strip and wax vinyl floors, to a high luster, using a non-slide finish
- Clean interior and exterior windows, (except front door and windows, to be done weekly)

Semi-annual:
- Wash Venetian blinds, return within two days of removal
- Wash the interior of all windows with Venetian blinds

Quality Assurance:
- Contractor will provide written record of monthly and quarterly quality checks to facility contact

Supplies:
- All items necessary to maintain quality cleaning and housekeeping is to be provided by the contractor including:

- Hand towels, multi-folded and roll type
- Toilet tissues, standard roll count of 1000 sheets per roll 4.5" x 4.5"
- Liquid hand soap
- Sanitary napkins
- Trash bags

Employee requirements:
- All employees must wear contractor's uniforms onsite, log-in daily and maintain proof of identification, bonding and insurance at all times.

Removal of employees:
- Contractor will remove any employee as requested by the facility administrator within 24 hrs of proper notice

Bonding and insurance:
- General business liability: NA
- Fidelity bond: NA
- Business automobile insurance (BAP): NA
- Surety bond: NA

Safety:
- Contractor will comply with all federal, state and local regulations including OSHA safety requirements
- Contractor will provide employees with proper PPE and safety training and ensure that safety signs are posted onsite as applicable.
- Contractor will provide MSDS's for all cleaning chemicals to be used, with the written bid proposal and as necessary, to the facility administrator, in advance of all substitutions

Terms:
Contract period:
- 1 year

Emergency maintenance rate:
- $10/hr for all non-routine cleaning work at the discretion of the facility administrator

Contracted cleaning rates:
- $0.08 per square foot per month
- $0.96 per square foot per year
- $1920 per month

Payment:
- Prices valid for life of contract
- Billing, 1st week of each month
- Payment within 30 days
- $25 processing fee on all returned checks

Performance based incentives*:
- Failure to perform all weekly and monthly services satisfactorily, and as scheduled, will result in a 10% deduction monthly, per occurrence.
- Failure to perform all monthly, quarterly and semi-annual, services satisfactorily, and as scheduled, will result in a 35% deduction, per

169

occurrence per time interval.

Contract extension:

- Service agreement may be extended for the period of 1 year, at the option of the facility administration and following completion of a service agreement extension and signatures from both the authorized facility management and the cleaning contractor's owner/ management.

Cancellation:

- The service agreement is subject to cancellation, at any time for lapse in performance of its terms and specification, by the contractor, as determined by the authorized agent of the "facility", or as warranted by unusual circumstances such as employee behavior or theft, substantive damage to facility personnel or property etc.,.

*These are, performance based contract, terms
and conditions. They are usually found in large
business and government contracts. They are
less common in small business service agreements.

ing services contract terms), presented here, shows examples of **pricing structures** for contracted cleaning services, that are expressed in terms common to many federal, state and local public agencies, namely:

- *price per square foot per month;*
- *price per square foot per year;*
- *total monthly cost;*
- *total annual cost.*

Many companies in the private sector, in particular, large corporations with regional, national, or global corporate infrastructures, may also expect bid proposals or quotes to be expressed or communicated in these terms.

In our example, the maximum cleaning rate of

Cleaning service rate calculations

(total monthly price) ÷ (cleanable surface area) =

(price per month per square foot)

and

(price per month per square foot) x 12 =

(price square per foot per year)

2,500 ft per square feet per person, is representative of actual janitorial service specifications, for routine or general office cleaning production rates and is a useful bench mark for estimating labor requirements. Minimum cleaning times or allowable production rates per employee, will vary depending on various factors, such as the number of occupants per square foot and the number of bathrooms, windows, carpet area, hard floor area, etc.,.

Some cleaning services specifications, may make other cleaning rate stipulations, such as a "minimum cleaning time", for facilities at, or under 2,000 sq. ft., that will be no less than 2 hours, etc.,. In other words, crews will be required to devote no less than two hours onsite, per cleaning interval.

Typical cleaning service rates

Janitorial and institutional housekeeping service rates, in both the public and private sector can vary from as little as $0.07 per square foot per month or less, to as high as $0.44 per square foot per month, or more, depending on the particular market, cleaning frequency, the types of cleaning and floor care services required, as well as such logistics as chemical or biological hazardous waste removal/ exposure, "clean room" specifications, etc.,. The typical range for these cleaning service rates, expressed in terms of an annual cost per foot, are $0.84 per sq. ft. per year to $5.28 per sq. ft. per year.

Professional floor care service rates are often quoted separately from routine cleaning services, particularly in the case of smaller businesses in the private sector. Floor care pricing, is subject to similar considerations, to that of routine office cleaning, such as the market or region, the number of floor finish coats, the cost of stripper and finish, the staging required (i.e., furniture removal, border taping, etc.,). For instance, some hard floor care professionals report rates varying from $0.12 to $0.35 per sq. ft., or more, for strip, wax and buffing services, depending these factors.

Pricing for carpet cleaning services can vary from ~$0.06-$0.21 per sq. ft., or more, based on the types of carpet and the services involved (i.e., carpet extraction, shampooing, bonnet cleaning, etc.,). Residential carpet cleaning services, frequently advertise special introductory discounts on their services through mailers, newspapers and broadcast media, etc.,.

For example, "any 3 rooms plus a hallway and set of steps, for $39 (3,000 sq. ft. max, wool, Berber, extra)", etc.,. This works out to somewhere on the order of $0.06-$0.07 per sq. ft., for typically sized rooms. Advertised prices for rotary carpet extraction systems may run from $0.12-$0.21 per sq. ft., or more.

Prices for specialty cleaning services such as window washing, Venetian blind cleaning, exterior pressure washing, are often quoted separately from basic cleaning services as well. Commercial Venetian blind cleaners for instance, charge on the order of $8-10 per blind, for same day service and will often use ultrasonic cleaning bath cleaning methods, to remove years of dirt and grime, in a matter of a minute or so. For a 6' x 2.5' blind, this works out to ~$0.50 per sq. ft.,.

Window washers may charge from $0.75-$5.00 per window or more, depending on such considerations, as the type of glass, the size of the window, whether both sides are cleaned, ease of access, etc.,.

A residential pressure washing service, may offer special introductory pricing, ranging from ~$90-$140 or more, for houses that vary in size from 2,500-5,000 sq. ft.,. This works out to ~$0.028-$0.036 per sq. ft.,.

It is usually best, to obtain as much information as possible about a prospective customer's cleaning specifications and pricing history or requirements, in advance of preparing a written bid proposal, or before providing a verbal quote. This is best accomplished through direct market research, such as information from purchasing agencies/ managers, research on local cleaning services advertising and feedback from customer surveys, etc.,. Each of these methods of research, should be a part of your marketing and bidding strategies, at some point.

Some useful charts for bid estimating and labor requirements, that are best suited for routine general office cleaning, are shown here. Charts for **cleanable surface area versus clean-**

ing time, are provided here. You can find an estimate, for the total time that it may take for general office cleaning, for cleanable surface areas ranging from 2,500-50,000 sq. ft., at a glance. Two production rates are provided, one for a single individual (2500 sq. ft. per hour per person), and one for a two man team (5000 sq. ft. per hour per two man team).

Using the two charts for **total price versus price per sq. ft. per month**, you can quickly calculate the monthly price to charge for a 2,500 sq. ft. cleanable surface area and a 5,000 sq. ft. cleanable surface area, based on the rate per sq. ft. per month.

It is important to remember that any formula, table, or software, used for calculating cleaning service bidding rates or price structures, is an approximation and should not preclude careful consideration of:

- *building specifications;*
- *cleaning specifications and logistics;*
- *the onsite walk through;*
- *special services such as floor care, window washing and Venetian blind cleaning;*

- *costs for overhead, labor, materials and supplies;*
- *customer pricing history.*

Whenever you are presented with a competitive situation, in which the current or recent price for a prospective client's cleaning services is known, you should <u>calculate</u> the lowest bid that you are prepared to offer, <u>prior</u> to negotiations (i.e., where possible). This is best accomplished, by estimating with adequate detail, your costs for overhead, labor, materials and supplies, to realistic minimums and then factoring in a profit margin, that is competitive and in keeping with your business goals.

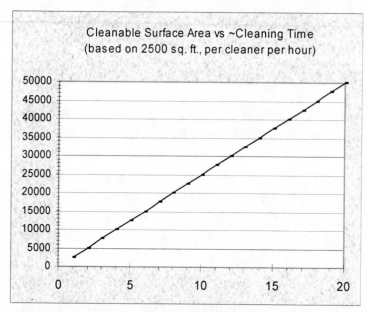

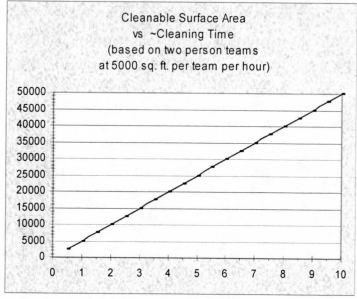

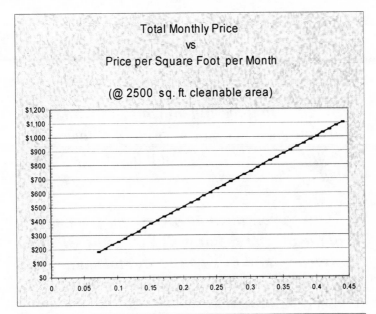

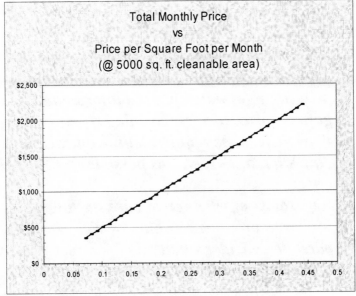

In closing, there are a number of points that should be made regarding the preceding discussion and examples.

- *Bidding on government contracts and in the private sector can be very competitive. The winning bid can vary from the next lowest bid by 5% or less.*

- *Many government agencies and companies in the private sector, will base their selection on more than price and may state additional criteria in pre-bid instructions or bidding specifications.*

- *To enhance your chances for a successful bid, prepare bid estimates with as much detail and quantitative precision as possible, integrating as much pre-bid information regarding price history, cleaning specifications, insurance requirements, contract/ bidding stipulations, etc., as possible.*

- *Regardless of whether you are starting a janitorial or home cleaning service, be prepared to consider whether a job or account is worth your time and in keeping with your goals and objectives, while avoiding a pattern of consistently noncompetitive pricing.*

There are a number of organizations, websites, internet bulletin boards, vendors, software and books, that may be useful in exploring the subjects of bidding, production rates and work loading, further. Several resources are listed here.

- **Cleaning management Institute**
  (articles & resources on cleaning)
  (www.cmmonline.com)
  1-518-783-1281

- **Building Service Contractors Association International**
  The Official BSCAI Guide to Bidding & Estimating
  (www.bscai.org or www.amazon.com (~$60)

- **Industry facts, figures and Trends**
  Donald E. Tepper, at (www.amazon.com) (~$160)

- **The NAPC Guide to Estimating Cleaning Services**
  (www.cleaningassocation.com)

- **Bidding and Estimating Janitorial Contracts**
  (www.janitorbooks.com)

- **(www.janitorialbidding.com)**
  sells books on bidding

- **Rim Rock Technologies software**
  at their website or at (www.cleanpro.com)
  bidding and bidding proposal software

- **NAPC bulletin board
  (www.cleaningassociation.com)**

- **(www.cleanlink.com) forum/bulletin board**

- **(www.windows101.com)
  bulletin board & specialty window
  cleaning equipment & supplies**

- **(www.window-cleaning-net.com)
  bulletin board**

Preparing and submitting a bid proposal

Once a company prepares a bid estimate, it follows logically, that the estimate must be communicated in some manner to prospective customers or clients. While it is always acceptable to provide a verbal quote, over the phone, or in person, particularly, when presented with urgency on the part of the customer, a verbal quote is usually followed-up by a <u>written</u> bid proposal.

A bid proposal can be sent via fax, mail, e-mail, or courier services, such as Fed-Ex (e.g., to ensure timely delivery and receipt by the appropriate person). Generally, a written bid proposal should include the following, as applicable:

- *an <u>introduction</u> that gets the attention of the reader and references, the reason or request that initiated the preparation of the bid proposal. For example, "As requested, following our recent phone conversation ...", or "As promised during the free onsite inspection and consultation that we provided recently, ..." etc.,);*

- *a discussion or reference that <u>addresses and explains specific solutions</u> to cleaning services problems or needs, that have been raised by the customer, in previous meetings or conversations;*

- *a brief <u>summary of the services</u> that will be provided, which is based on the pricing structure quoted in the bid proposal. Standard services, with prices and options, as well as any special pricing considerations, should be listed as well;*

- *the <u>Terms and conditions</u> of the services to be provided, such as the "What, where and when?", of the services that will be provided for the prices quoted and stipulations for contract extensions, cancellation of services,* *insurance, payment etc.;*

- *a <u>conclusion</u> or "outro", which indicates the steps and contact information, necessary for the client to enter into a service agreement (Here you can also include, brief testimonials from loyal customers, or facts and statistics concerning your business, such as insurance and bonding information, that establish your business's credibility);*

- *a <u>closing statement</u> , thanking the prospective customer for his or her time and consideration.*

A standard contract or service agreement, which has been reviewed by appropriate legal counsel, may be included with the proposal. It should be written in such a way, as to reference the bid proposal. After the customer accepts your bid, each party should receive a copy of the bid proposal, along with any <u>signed</u> contract or agreement that is used. When a bid proposal is the sole record that defines price, method of payment, along with the specific terms and conditions of the services to be provided, the proposal then becomes part of the agreement or contract, once it is signed.

Alternatively, the bid proposal, or portions thereof, may serve as the service agreement or contract. For example, an attachment to the bid proposal could be prepared in simple and clear language, that explicitly restates the essential elements of the bid proposal. Such a document should have provisions for signatures and dates (i.e., for both parties) and might define at a minimum:

- *the cleaning specifications, including cleaning task descriptions, frequency, acceptable levels of quality and which party is responsible for supplies;*
- *payment terms including price method and schedule;*
- *terms of contract length, along with provisions for extensions and cancellations;*
- *provisions for non-routine or emergency service;*
- *other terms and conditions that define responsibilities, such as building access and recourse in the event of unforeseen or unexpected problems or liability, such as employee behavior, nonperformance of ser-*

> **vices, theft, property damage, personal injury** *(e.g., references to the insurance coverage maintained by your cleaning service, on an item by item basis, i.e., for theft, property damage, etc., as applicable).*

The NOA example presented earlier, may serve as a good starting point for drafting such a document.

Many small business and residential customers may not expect to enter into, or expect to sign a written agreement. Failure to secure a document with signatures, that grants your company authorized access to a customer's facility and assigns responsibilities for liability, may put you at substantial risk for a law suit, or prosecution, under the wrong circumstances.

This is particularly true, when you are engaging the services of employees or independent contractors, which increases your risk of liability for damages or prosecution. Obtaining the advice of appropriate legal counsel and cleaning services professionals in your area, regarding potential liabilities and the relevant laws that apply in your state or province, is advised prior to drafting a generic cleaning service agreement, or prior to signing any agreements drafted by the customer.

A template for a bid proposal, with many of the basic elements previously discussed, is presented here. In this example, a bid proposal is introduced and explained to a prospective client and then a reference to a general service agreement (not shown), is made.

The approach that you select, may be longer or shorter, depending on the services that you are providing and the detail with which you wish to convey the various components of your bid proposal. If your proposal exceeds one page, it may be helpful to use both sides of a page to reduce the amount of paper the customer has to thumb through (i.e., for economy of presentation).

Notice that the example provided here, serves as a sales and promotional tool, as well. It points to the details of <u>specific solutions</u> for existing problems and provides an overview of the credentials of the company and its employees. Making such points, could prove to be the deciding factor, in receiving a favorable outcome from your proposal. They also accomplish the important goal of helping to distinguish your company from its competitors.

Acme Janitorial, Inc.
XXX Any street,
Any town, Any state/province
zip or mailing code: xxxxxx
Phone: xxx-xxx-xxxx
e-mail@acme.com
www.acme.com

Date: xx/xx/xx

To: "Responsible facility contact"
Customer/ Business's name
Customer/ Business's address

Re: Bid proposal for cleaning services

Dear Mr./ Ms. "Responsible facility contact",

It was a pleasure meeting with you recently (*actual date optional*), to discuss your cleaning needs, during our free inspection and onsite consultation
(*you may reference a recent phone conversation, or other type of meeting
instead of an onsite consultation, here, as well*). As you requested, Acme
janitorial, Inc., has prepared a quote for cleaning services, that we feel is
very competitive for the services to be provided and will best meet your
cleaning needs for the future.

We have prepared our proposal with special consideration for the following
cleaning needs that you have expressed interest in, as well as the problems
that you are currently experiencing with your present service:

Cleaning needs:
- Routine general office cleaning
- Hard floor care maintenance program
- Carpet care maintenance program

Problems or concerns:
- Spotty or inconsistent general office cleaning
  (e.g., waste baskets left full, carpets left un-vacuumed)
- Dust build-up and waste container overflow
- Doors left unsecured

- Lights left on or turned off, other than as specified by the customer
- Poor quality of hard floor care (e.g., low luster, slippery finish)
- Carpet stains allowed to stand and degrade the carpets

To address these issues we are recommending the following services and practices, to most effectively meet your cleaning needs and minimize or eliminate the problems you are currently experiencing.

Routine general office cleaning:
3 times weekly (Tuesday, Thursday, weekend)
- Vacuum, or damp mopping of all floor surfaces
- Dusting of all desks, chairs, cabinets, tables and ledges
- Clean and disinfect bathroom toilet and sink fixtures
- Clean bathroom mirrors and wet mop bathroom floors
- Empty all ashtrays and trash receptacles as specified by the customer
- Clean front door glass and adjoining windows (inside and out)

Monthly deep clean to include:
- Wet mopping of all hard floors
- Spot cleaning of carpets and hard floors and for deep scuffs and stains
- Detailed cleaning of break room appliance surfaces as specified by the customer
- Thorough dusting of all surfaces as specified in routine office cleaning, as well as conspicuous or problem build-up areas as specified by the customer (via instructions left at the front desk)

Quarterly hard floor care maintenance to include;
- an initial stripping and refinish of all hard floors, using a high luster finish formulation with anti-slide additives (the use of a special formulation, coupled with the use of a high speed burnisher, will ensure a near "wet look" luster or finish)
- Monthly maintenance of hard floor surfaces to include cleaning or scrubbing of high traffic or problem areas
- Monthly spray buffing of reception area, break room, as well as high traffic or problem areas, susceptible to de-lustering, as needed.

Carpet maintenance program to include:
- Monthly, or as needed, spot cleaning of high traffic or problem areas
- Quarterly carpet extraction of all high traffic and problem areas
- Semi-annual carpet extraction with deodorizer treatment

Cleaning and housekeeping supplies:
- Acme janitorial will provide all cleaning supplies and trash can liners needed to perform the cleaning services to be provided
- Extra liners will be placed at the bottom of each trash receptacle to provide for in-house trash removal, between regularly scheduled cleaning services, in the event of potential overflow (should the problem persist, larger waste containers, or a move to daily cleaning service is recommended)
- All other housekeeping including, but not limited to, toilet paper, paper towels, hand soap, deodorizers, etc., will be provided by the customer

In addition, the attending general cleaning and floor care technicians will complete and initial a daily checklist, to include routine cleaning tasks performed, as well as a check to ensure that all doors are secured and the lighting is left as specified by the customer. A copy will be left for the facility contact at the front desk and their attending supervisor. This will help to monitor our performance and help to ensure that your existing cleaning service problems are minimized or eliminated.

Acme janitorial, Inc., provides complete window washing, Venetian blind washing, exterior pressure washing and gutter cleaning services as well. A brochure describing all of our standard services, is provided with this proposal (*attaching a brochure is optional*).

We are pleased to offer these services to you at the competitive rates listed below. The prices quoted are good for 30 days from the date of this proposal. Billing is on the 1st of the month, unless otherwise requested by the customer, and is payable by check within 30 days. There is a $25 service charge, for processing all returned checks (*billing stipulations are optional, they may be listed in the service agreement, as well*).

Routine cleaning services: **$ XXX. XX/ mo**

Carpet care maintenance program: **$ XXX. XX/ mo**

COMMERCIAL & RESIDENTIAL CLEANING SERVICES

Hard floor care maintenance program: **$ XXX. XX/ mo**
Emergency or non-routine services: **$XX/ hr**
(includes all labor and basic cleaning supplies)

A copy of the proposed services and price quotes, as well as terms and conditions, are attached with a general service agreement that we provide to all of our customers.

Acme Janitorial, Inc., is an equal opportunity employer, serving our community since XXXX. Each of our technicians is professionally trained, fully bonded and insured, wears a uniform with an identifiable Acme janitorial logo or insignia and carries personal identification and proof of insurance at all times. We are also proud member of such prominent professional cleaning industry associations, as the NAPC, BCSAI and the IICRC.

We would like to thank you for your interest in Acme, at this time. To enter into a service agreement, complete the attached billing information form and provide an authorized signature on the general service agreement. Then phone or e-mail our offices and one of our account representatives will call on you within 2 business days, to pick-up copies of the contract, receive building access instructions, and answer any questions you may have regarding our services, at that time.

If you have any questions regarding our company, or you wish to discuss additional services, or changes to our proposal, please don't hesitate to call.

Sincerely,

Your Name, owner/ operator

Acme Janitorial, Inc.
XXX Any street,
Any town, Any state/province
zip or mailing code: xxxxxx
Phone: xxx-xxx-xxxx
e-mail@acme.com
www.acme.com

Negotiations with clients

Price and contract negotiations can be defined, first as a part of fundamental business communications and secondly, as an extension of the basic marketing, advertising and sales process.

Throughout our daily lives, it seems that we are continually shopping for, or negotiating for some type of advantage or concessionary haste, in order to improve or enhance the quality of our lives. For example, we may request the largest or most appealing portion or item, at a bakery or a produce stand. We routinely shop for the best price and warranty on a car or appliance. We negotiate our salaries and often, our benefits. We search for the best deal for airline tickets and then for a seating position, or upgrade to our liking and so on.

The process of inquiry and requests for the best price, position, salary, item in a lot or group, etc., is at its roots, a part of fundamental business communications.

The components involved in a job search, such as preparing and submitting resumes, interview-

ing and negotiating salaries and benefits, are examples of business communication processes.
They are familiar to most everyone and bear
striking similarities to the processes involved in
starting a business (e.g., determining a target
market, advertising, establishing price structures,
or preparing and submitting a bid proposal and
negotiating a price or service agreement).

For instance, to begin a job search, we have to
decide what type of field we want to pursue,
then we have to possess, or acquire the tools and
skills sets necessary to be marketable. We might
then select a target market within our chosen
field, based on such factors as the geographical
area, proximity to our present home and immediate family members or relatives, the size of the
market (e.g., relative number of job openings),
the highest salary range, the best chance for success, based on our skill sets, etc.,.

For example, a chef living in New York who is
trained in authentic French cuisine, may likely
target the top French restaurants within commut-
ing distance, to send his resumes to first.
The next step in his job search, is to determine
the relative value of his services, which is simi-

lar to the process of establishing <u>price structures</u> or <u>bid estimates</u> for cleaning services.

To do this, he researches the internet for salary norms in his field, combs through newspaper advertisements and also polls his peers. He also tallies his <u>overhead</u> expenses, such as his school loan, rent, utilities, insurance, transportation, food, clothing, etc., and establishes a basis for the minimum compensation he will need for his services.

These activities are similar to the processes that a business engages in, specifically, <u>market research</u> and <u>bid estimating</u>, or <u>price structuring</u>. The next step in our chef's job search, is to prepare a resume´ that communicates his credentials and what services that he can provide to a prospective employer, such as food preparation skills, dishes that he specializes in, culinary training, restaurant experience etc.,.

Our chef's resume´ is essentially an <u>advertisement</u> of his skills and is similar to many <u>bid proposals,</u> in that it communicates what services he is offering and is distributed to his <u>target market,</u> usually in response to their need or request (e.g., in response to a help wanted sign or classified job ad).

Just as many janitorial services may not disclose their pricing in advertisements, or over the phone, our chef may opt, not to disclose his salary history or requirements, until a personal interview has been completed.

A job interview is similar in many ways to an onsite consultation, that may be conducted by a janitorial or home cleaning service. In this case, once he lands a job interview, our chef has to determine the employer's needs and demonstrate to the employer, that his services are the best solution for meeting those needs.

After an inspection of the restaurant and receiving an overview from the owner, concerning the current needs in the kitchen area, the chef may offer, or be invited to provide a demonstration of his cooking skills, by preparing a dish for the restaurant owner or the head chef*. As mentioned earlier in this book, the chef's demonstration, as with offering to perform an initial cleaning, is a common method of soliciting business and determining a price for one's services.

*Note: some cleaning service professionals report that performing casual demonstrations, such as spot cleaning of carpets or hard floors, can be effective in displaying skills and establishing credibility during onsite consultations.

Our chef chooses to demonstrate the preparation of two dishes, an entrée that is not on the menu and the restaurant's most popular entrée. The chef chooses these two dishes to demonstrate his skills in meeting the current needs of his customer (i.e., the restaurant owner or manager) and to display his specialty or specialized services (i.e., his specialty dish, that is not on the menu).

The chef's demonstration is a continuation of the advertising and sales process*. Preparing the most popular dish on the restaurant's menu, is clearly, the ultimate "road test" of his skills. Also, by presenting an additional dish that is not on the menu, he is providing to the restaurant owner, an entrée that may enhance the restaurant's business. This "second" demonstration, is both an advertisement and a potential negotiating tool, provided that his cooking skills are equal to the challenge.

*Note: a demonstration that might be used by a janitorial service, would be an offer to strip, wax and buff a small area, such as a reception area, using a high speed burnisher, in order to demonstrate the added value of a "wet look" floor finish. A home cleaning service might offer a deep clean, or a specialized service such as cleaning the inside of an oven or refrigerator, or a window cleaning, inside and out, etc.,.

The chef notices during the demonstration, that the volume in the restaurant is quite high and notes this, both as a reason to raise his <u>minimum salary requirements</u> and as a potential <u>bargaining tool</u> during negotiations. Additionally, he sees a potential for reorganizing how the food orders are routed, as well as how food ingredients are staged and then prepared, that would greatly improve efficiency. Again he takes note and now has yet another potential tool for <u>negotiation</u>.

The restaurant's owner and its head chef are favorably impressed by both of the dishes our chef has prepared, but because of the keen competition among French chefs in the New York area, they offer him a position with a salary that is below his desired range and just above his minimum salary requirements.

Privately, our chef is prepared to accept the salary if he must, but <u>politely and eloquently</u> pleads his case for compensation, closer to his desired salary range. He appeals to the Restaurant owner by stating his strong points. He is a graduate of the most prestigious French cooking school in the world, his references as a chef's assistant, are from the best restaurants in Paris, and   he has reputation for consistency and promptness in food preparation, under high customer volume conditions.

He adds, that the scraps from the preparation of both of his dishes were a "hit" with the kitchen staff and a long time patron of the restaurant, who happened to be chatting with the staff at the time. Finally, he further distinguishes himself from other chefs competing for the job, by <u>politely and modestly</u> sharing his observations for improving the kitchen's efficiency.

The restaurant owner is moved by our chef's insight into the workings of the restaurant's operations and is impressed by his credentials, as well as the potential for our chef's special entrée, to increase the restaurant's business. The owner whispers to the head chef and then offers our chef a salary that is at the high end of his desired salary range.

The point of our analogy, is not to show that one must always hold out for the highest price possible. It is to show how every aspect of our chef's efforts to land a job is ultimately a part of, or a continuation of the process of <u>marketing</u>, <u>advertising</u> and <u>sales</u>. In effect, he is "selling his skills" to the restaurant owner.

A closer look at our idealized example, uncovers similarities between our chef's job search and basic techniques and strategies, that are used to negotiate a price for products or services, close on a customized service agreement proposal, or to land a contract to provide standard services at a predetermined price.

Here are some of these techniques or strategies.

- *Offering to demonstrate a product or service*

- *Demonstrating basic features or services needed by the customer, as well as special features or services that may be valued by the customer*

- *The use of references or testimonials to establish or enhance the credibility of products or services*

- *Offering <u>choices</u>, for specialized products and services, in addition to basic products and services*

- *Using observations of the client's needs or problems, to offer potential solutions within the scope of your product or services*

- *Stressing the greater or long term benefits of a product or service, beyond its obvious utility*

- *Anticipation, or prior knowledge of the range between breakeven and a realistic premium for products or services in a targeted market*

- *Careful and <u>tempered</u> delivery of each point of negotiation*

- *Entering into negotiations with clearly defined objectives for:*

- ◆   *the minimum price or service rate, you will offer or accept;*
- ◆   *a target, for a competitive or premium price for your services; and*
- ◆   *counter offer strategies that add extras, or specialized products and services, to offset reduced profit margins, on an initial offer made by the customer, for basic or core products and services*

Many specific ideas on negotiating a price for services, or the terms of a service agreement, have been expressed in the example of the chef's job search, and throughout this guide. For instance, the bid proposal example presented the preceding section, employs several of the above techniques and strategies for negotiating a price for your services and closing on a service agreement.

In the example of a bid proposal presented earlier, the careful use of "bullet points" to outline proposed cleaning solutions to each of the customer's specific problems, demonstrates an intent on the part of the janitorial services contractor, to meet the customer's needs. It also serves as a reminder to the customer that each of his current cleaning service problems were carefully considered and cost effective solutions put forth.

The bid proposal also shows an intent to offer solutions with the customer's "pocket book" in mind, by providing three progressive options or solutions for the problem of trash container overflows. Namely, it offers provisions for additional trash liners, for in-house or "self-service" use, a recommendation to purchase waste receptacles with a larger capacity and finally, the option to expand services to a daily regime.

These techniques and strategies can be used effectively at most any step in the process of marketing, advertising and sales of your company's cleaning services (e.g., during price and contract negotiations). They are useful in face to face negotiations, written communications, as well as conversations over the phone. For example, a caller leaves a message in response to a flyer or door hanger, recently distributed on your business's behalf.

After learning somewhat about this potential residential customer's needs over the phone, you return the customer's call, but she is not in. You decide to leave a targeted voice mail, that suggests a cost effective solution to her cleaning needs on a biweekly basis, as opposed to the weekly service that she is now receiving.

This advice, "segways" into an invitation for an onsite consultation and initial cleaning. The point here, is that even in the midst of telephone tag, which is common and all too often, unavoidable, there is an opportunity to provide information to prospective clients, that will lead them to make the decision to meet with you, or employ your services outright.

Finally, when negotiating with prospective customers or existing clients, it is important to keep the customer's needs in focus, know what your services are worth at a minimum and avoid appearing desperate, boastful, or intimidating.

Chapter 6

Cleaning practices, safety and customer relations

In this chapter, we will discuss three topics that are important, once you have landed your first clients. Maintaining good **customer relations** is essential to the <u>continued</u> success of any service based business and cleaning services are no exception. Proper **safety practices** are needed to protect both employees and customers from harm or injury. Additionally, many occupational safety practices are <u>required</u> and are regulated by federal state and local laws, in particular by OSHA, the federal government's occupational safety and health administration. Attention to detail and the use of established **cleaning practices**, are absolutely essential to maintaining a high level of quality and efficiency, <u>consistently</u>.

Cleaning practices

Implementing cleaning practices that ensure a consistent level of quality and efficiency, will go a long way towards:

- *establishing good customer relations and keeping valued customers or accounts;*

- *maintaining your profit margins, through consistent and efficient execution of services;*

- *enhancing your business's reputation, leading to its further growth.*

Attention to detail, consistency and **efficiency** are essential components of good cleaning practices. These components, combined with specific knowledge of the appropriate cleaning materials and equipment for cleaning processes such as carpet extraction, stripping, scrubbing and buffing, window washing, spot removal, etc., will help prevent you from losing accounts due to spotty or inconsistent work. They will also help you maintain or improve your profit margins and when integrated with effective training and supervision, good cleaning practices can help to reduce employee turnover and improve employee moral.

Many resources for learning about basic cleaning techniques and specialized cleaning services such as carpet care and hard floor care, window washing, etc., have been cited in earlier chapters. A careful search at your local library, or on the internet, can provide additional information on specific cleaning materials techniques. Some resources that may be useful and worth exploring are presented here.

- **The Cleaning Encyclopedia (a professional guide to cleaning everything from A-Z), Don Aslett, ~$6.29 at (www.amazon.com)**

- **(www.doityourself.com) cleaning tips and cleaning forum**

- **(www.frugalitynetwork.com) provides links to house cleaning tips**

- **Clean your house safely and effectively: without harmful chemicals, Randy Dunford, ~$9.95 at (www.opengroup.com)**

- **The IEHA, International Executive Housekeepers Association (www.ieha.org) provides certification and registration for institutional cleaners and supervisors**

- **500 Terrific ideas for cleaning everything:** expert advice from choosing supplies to cleaning absolutely everything, Don Aslett, ~$6.95 at (www.opengroup.com)

- Mary Findley's (www.goclean.com) Cleaning tips and monthly newsletters related to cleaning

- (www.about.com) focus on PC support cleaning tips for cleaning PC's, without damaging them

- (www.a2zcarpet.com) carpet care guide, stain removal guide

- **Cleaning performance handbook** Gary Clipperson at (www.nationalproclean.com)

Attention to details, such as the presence of heel marks (sometimes these can be removed by a pencil eraser), dust balls*, carpet stains, window or mirror streaks, finger marks or smudges, as well as dust build-up* on such surfaces as telephones, computers, ledges, heating and air conditioning vents, fire extinguishers, etc., may prevent a complaint, that often leads very rapidly to the loss of an account. One standard practice that can help here, is to perform a deep clean at least monthly, with an emphasis on dirt and dust build-up and any other problem areas that need attention.

*(these dust culprits can cause you to lose an account almost as fast as they form!)

Another very helpful technique, is to maintain a checklist, to help ensure the detection and elimi- nation of these dirt and soil items. Checklists can also be used to monitor and help ensure the satisfactory completion of all basic and special- ized services performed at each account. The use of checklists helps to ensure that nothing is forgotten or overlooked and it can also be used as a record to monitor employee performance.

This approach, also promotes a professional im- age with customers and employees. Maintaining such records and correcting problems in a timely manner, is a fundamental form of quality control or assurance. Some type of quality assurance activity or program, is often required by large commercial and government accounts.

Many of these organizations will score the qual- ity of your services using guidelines defined in service agreements or using commercial com- puter software. If you are bound by a performance based contract, your company may be subject to severe payment penalties for each occurrence of nonperformance, or inadequate quality of service. In other cases you may simply lose the business altogether.

Consistency, is perhaps the most critical element in developing and observing good cleaning practices. It is important to realize that the cleaning services industry is very competitive and that in the case of commercial janitorial or institutional housekeeping accounts, there may be dozens or hundreds of individuals that can provide feedback to the facility contact, each with a different viewpoint, as to what level of service is being provided.

Glaring or obvious breaches in services, such as failing to vacuum, sweep or dust mop floors, failure to clean bathroom fixtures, or restock housekeeping supplies and perhaps most importantly, failing to empty waste baskets or other trash receptacles, may go unnoticed by a single individual, but are unlikely to escape the attention of everyone. To prevent these lapses in service from occurring, it is important, to learn to perform cleaning tasks in a logical, orderly, ergonomic and <u>reproducible</u> manner.

For instance, vacuuming, sweeping and mopping should follow the emptying of trash where possible, in order to avoid trash debris from hitting a floor after it has been cleaned. Cleaning from the highest point to the lowest point in a room, is a good rule of thumb here.

Secondly, you should always stage your cleaning equipment materials and housekeeping supplies, such as trash liners and paper products on caddies or carts, in advance of performing cleaning tasks in a given area, wherever possible. This will help to ensure that each cleaning or supply replacement task, has been thought of in advance and will be completed satisfactorily during the course of the cleaning routine. This will also improve cleaning efficiency.

Proper staging of equipment and materials is an ergonomic approach, that will minimize wasted travel around the facility or home being cleaned and will help to ensure that a task such as re-stocking toilet paper or liquid soap, is not forgotten. Using a checklist for each cleaning task that is performed and maintaining an <u>inventory</u> of cleaning and housekeeping supplies, will help to prevent any lapse in cleaning services. Running to the 24 hour convenience mart for emergency supplies, can be costly in terms of time and money. This also may not be an option, if for example, you are cleaning a facility in the early morning hours and discover a shortage of supplies, just prior to occupancy by the tenants.

The more orderly a cleaning pattern or a set of work instructions, for a group of cleaning tasks is, the easier that it will be to commit even the smallest of details to memory. Cleaning patterns and work instructions must be logical and straightforward so that they can be implemented correctly and performed consistently. Through thoughtful repetition, production rates or cleaning efficiencies will also improve significantly.

Common sense cleaning routines, that employ the use of logical cleaning patterns, such as circular or clockwise cleaning paths, or the practice of making a final pass to inspect sections or areas which have been cleaned, will help to ensure that all basic cleaning tasks are completed satisfactorily. If you have ever had occasion to move yourself or your family, then you already know how important, the order and manner in which you pack household items onto a moving van or truck, may be, in order to get all of your belongings moved as safely and efficiently as possible. The principle for establishing logical and efficient cleaning patterns is much the same.

Cleaning practices such as:

- *leaving a uniform pattern to a carpet's pile through the use of sequential vacuum "strokes" or passes;*
- *polishing bathroom and kitchen fixture chrome surfaces;*
- *folding the top flap of restocked tissue paper to a point;*
- *applying a bathroom deodorizer;*
- *leaving extra trash liners underneath the one in use;*
- *orienting chairs in a uniform pattern;*
- *arranging throw rugs uniformly;*
- *closing all internal doors or returning the lighting to its required status as specified by the customer, etc.,*

are all useful or helpful ways of leaving the customer with the clear impression that basic cleaning services have been performed thoroughly and unobtrusively. In some cases, they may even be a part of the customer's requirements or cleaning specifications.

Team based cleaning techniques, similar to concepts or approaches used in professional sports, such as "flooding a zone", "man to man" or "zone defenses", are commonly employed by many cleaning services, particularly in the case of crews working in large facilities.

For instance, one approach that is analogous to "flooding a zone" with defenders or receivers in football, is to disperse an entire crew or portions thereof, into a problem area or zone (i.e., with redundancy or depth for each basic task, such as vacuuming, or dusting, etc.,), followed by a "sweep" of the area to ensure thoroughness and to address problem spots, or to perform more specialized or labor intensive tasks.

An approach that is similar to a "man to man" coverage or defense, used in basketball and football, or the use of a starting, middle inning reliever and closing relief pitchers in baseball, is to have dedicated "experts" for each type of cleaning task such as vacuuming, dusting, sweeping, cleaning bathrooms, cleaning windows, emptying trash, etc.,. Each expert or specialist plays a specific role in a cleaning routine. This approach may also be useful in the management of employees, who show a predisposition or skill, for one cleaning task or another. Rotating cleaning roles, is another team cleaning option, that can also promote fairness and teamwork.

Finally, an approach similar to a "zone defense", used in basketball and football, is to divide the facility into zones (e.g., each floor of a multi-floor building, etc.,) and make each person responsible for all cleaning tasks, in that zone.

The proper use of these cleaning practices can greatly improve efficiencies or production rates for cleaning tasks. Some industry professionals report improvements in production rates of 30%-40% or more, through the use of some of these team based techniques.

It is also worth noting while discussing team based cleaning concepts, that in 1998 the Occupational Outlook handbook, stated that only 1 in 20 cleaning industry employees is a supervisor and the average income for a college educated supervisor or manager, was ~$37,000/ year. The use of team based cleaning concepts and quality assurance methods, such as cleaning task checklists, that are signed and submitted by employees after each shift, may help to limit the amount of supervisory personnel needed for your business.

Safety practices

A safe working environment is necessary to protect both employees and customers from harm or injury and in order to comply with federal, state and local laws. This can be achieved through measures such as the proper use of personal protection equipment (PPE), proper safety training (e.g., hazard communications and the use of MSDS sheets), engineering controls (e.g., proper ventilation, safety guards, etc.,), appropriate and timely posting of safety signs and through compliance with all pertinent OSHA regulations.

A complete discussion of safety requirements for a small business, is outside the scope of this guide. You should plan to educate yourself adequately and seek professional advice as necessary, in order to be in compliance with the "laws of the land" and to ensure the safety of your employees and customers.

OSHA publishes regulations and reporting forms, as well as statistics regarding the most frequent noncompliance violations, categorized by the relative size of a business, based on the number of employees it has. OSHA provides this information through their website (**www.osha.gov**), regional offices and small entity (i.e., small business) compliance guides. Some of the safety forms, posters, safety guides and industry statistics, that may be useful to your business, can be downloaded from the OSHA website, or ordered through their website and regional offices. Some of these publications are listed here.

- *__Handbook for Small Businesses__ (OSHA publication 2209);*

- *__Hazard Communication Guideline__ __for Compliance__ (OSHA publication 3111);*

- *__Keeping Your Workplace Safe__ (OSHA brochure-flyer);*

- *__Assessing the Need for Personal Protection Equip-__*

*ment (A Guide for Small Business Employers)
(OSHA publication 3151);*

- *Chemical Hazard Communication
  (OSHA publication 3084);*

- *Personal protective Equipment*
  (OSHA publication 3077)

- *Small Businesses– Questions & Answers*
  (OSHA publication 3163)

Some of the regulations that are most likely to be pertinent to a janitorial or institutional housekeeping start-up, at some point in its development, are:

- *Hazard communications;*
- *MSDS employee access and right to know;*
- *Safety labeling for regulated chemicals;*
- *Personal protective equipment (PPE)* (e.g., eye, hands, head, feet, back and respiratory);
- *Confined space entry;*
- *Occupational injury & illness recording and reporting* (OSHA form 200*);
- *Workman's compensation;*
- *Hazardous waste operations;*
- *Bloodborne pathogens* (exposure control);
- *Means of egress;*

- ***Lockout tag-out.***
Some of the most important and practical safety measures, that most any sized cleaning business should implement, at a <u>minimum</u> (i.e., where appropriate), are:

- *timely posting of safety signs in floor areas with wet surfaces, or where hazardous chemicals, such as some floor stripping formulations and cleaning solvents are present, posing a respiratory hazard, as well as in areas where equipment and materials present a hazard to passers by;*

- *prohibit the placement of equipment and materials that block means of egress (i.e., doorways, exit pathways, etc.,);*

- *the use of proper PPE, when handling potentially hazardous cleaning chemicals, where heavy lifting is involved, in areas where construction is ongoing, or where moving equipment is being used;*

- *proper labeling of all containers containing regulated or harmful chemicals, including utility spray bottles;*

- *providing <u>documented</u> hazard communications to employees, as well as maintaining MSDS sheets for regulated chemicals and making them available to employees and customers;*

- *observing standard safety precautions when using sharp, heavy, electrical, or motorized equipment, including lock-out, tag-out procedures (i.e., signs/tags and procedures that prevent the use of malfunctioning equipment, or prevents employees from turning on electrical power where other employees may be at risk of electrical shock);*

- *observing standard safety precautions when handling or using regulated or potentially hazardous cleaners and floor care chemicals, such as proper ventilation and the use of eye, hand and respiratory personal protective equipment (PPE), as well as avoiding the <u>mixing</u>, or simultaneous use of <u>incompatible</u> <u>chemicals</u> (e.g., acids and bases, ammonia and bleach, etc.,);*

- *prohibiting employees from eating, drinking*

or smoking in the presence of hazardous chemicals, biological hazards and flammable substances;

- *avoiding unsafe practices, such as overloading electrical outlets, placing equipment and supplies on ladders, etc., as well as removing sources of ignition from the vicinity of flammable chemicals;*

- *proper training and the use of appropriate PPE, for the handling and disposal of biohazards (i.e., blood, human or animal tissues and other potentially infectious bodily fluids, sharps and shards) and hazardous materials and chemicals (e.g., mercury from broken thermometers, etc.,);*

- *maintaining records and reporting occupational injuries and illnesses using OSHA form 200*, as well as providing workman's compensation insurance, as applicable.*

*Employers with 10 or less employees and some types of businesses may be exempt from keeping OSHA form 200 records.

Many of these safety measures are common sense, whereas other measures will require additional research and study, in order to learn whether and when, each safety regulation applies to your situation and how to comply with each of them.

For example, an MSDS, is a material safety data sheet. They provide data and information on appropriate labeling, PPE (personal protective equipment), fire extinguishing media, engineering controls, toxicity and disposal methods for regulated materials that pose a potential hazard to the users or the environment.

OSHA regulations basically state that employers must maintain copies of MSDS sheets, for all regulated materials that they have in their possession and make them available to employees, contractors and visitors, working with, or exposed to these materials (in this case your customers may be entitled to access, or may require you to provide copies of MSDS sheets for all of these materials).

The manufacturers of your cleaning chemicals

are required to insert them into product packaging. If you call, e-mail or write the manufacturer, they will send you a copy of the MSDS (often some proof of purchase, such as a purchase order number, is required as well). A number of commercial MSDS and safety information websites, such as **www.msdsonline.com, www.msdssearch.com** and **www.chesnet.com**, provide searchable databases for MSDS sheets, on thousands of generic chemicals, as well.

There are also many on-line resources, for training and educating yourself and your employees regarding OSHA safety regulations, that may be applicable to your particular situation. Some safety training websites such as **www.free-training.com** and **www.natlenvtrainers.com** (national environmental trainers), provide on-line introductory training as well as fully accredited safety training for certifying both employees and trainers, on such compliance issues as bloodborne pathogens (i.e., exposure control), hazardous waste operations, hazard communications, PPE and so on.

If your employees are exposed to biohazards, or handle and dispose of biohazardous wastes, they must be properly trained regarding bloodborne pathogens (biological material containing potentially infectious substances), as required by what OSHA calls "Exposure Control" regulations. They must also be provided with proper PPE.

Some examples of cleaning situations in which these regulations <u>may</u> be applicable to your business, are nursing homes, hospitals, biological laboratories, blood donation centers, funeral homes, some doctor's and dentist's offices, etc.,.

Even in general office cleaning where exposure to bloodborne pathogens is minimal, employees should be instructed to observe "Universal Precautions", by avoiding direct contact to the eyes, nose, mouth, or skin, with human blood or any other bodily fluids, as well as with excretions such as fecal matter, urine, vomit or sputum. Proper use of disinfectants, and PPE, such as non-porous gloves, like Platex gloves, when cleaning bathroom floors, toilets, urinals and sinks, are useful precautions, when cleaning bathrooms, or in other cleaning situations, where there is exposure to potentially infectious substances (e.g., cleaning up blood spots or vomit, etc.,).

Customer relations

Good customer relations practices, are essential to maintaining a smooth working relationship with customers, <u>keeping</u> their business and towards establishing a reputation among clients that helps to grow your business. Some findings from a study by Technical Assistance Research Programs, Inc., (TARP), (i.e., "Consumer Complaint Handling in America"), illustrates the point very clearly:

- *"~50% of the time, customers who have a problem with a product or service are not likely to tell the provider about it";*

- *"nine out of ten of these "silent critics" will probably take their future business to a competitor";*

- *"dissatisfied customers tell between seven to nine other people about unsatisfactory experiences with a company or its products";*

- *"word of mouth, is one of the most important factor in a company's decision to buy*

products and services for its operations".
It is important to train all of your employees, on
how to conduct themselves around customers
and how to respond to customer complaints and
inquiries. They represent the company and its
image, at all times and this is perhaps the first
and foremost instruction, to provide to them.
Some fundamentals of customer relations are
presented here. They are applicable to employers and employees in any business ranging from
a solo start-up, to a fortune 500 company.

- *every employee is a representative of the
  company and contributes directly its image,
  each employee should act accordingly on
  the job, at all times;*

- *each employee should always observe basic
  "fundamentals of business interactions",
  such as a genuine smile and direct eye contact, when greeting customers (this includes
  all of the customer's employees, as well as
  visitors onsite);*

- *respond to all customer complaints and inquiries, as <u>promptly</u> and <u>courteously</u> as possible, referring them to a supervisor as nec-*

essary (uncompleted or unsatisfactory follow-up to customer complaints and inquiries = lost business and a poor reputation among customers);

- *supervisors and employees alike, should assess customer complaint situations personally, wherever appropriate, in order to provide accurate and detailed feedback to managers and to demonstrate diligence to the customer, in responding to their requests;*

- *avoid negative or indifferent behavior, speech, or lines of reasoning. If an employee does not know how to answer a customer's question, they should promise to fulfill their request by referring the question to a supervisor or manager;*

- *always observe the old adage that "the customer is always right" and avoid confrontation at all times.*

Some companies provide their employees with instructional tools, such as foldout cards that have their quality policies, mission statements, or other company policies and information on them. Including or summarizing some of these customer relations fundamentals, on such cards, can provide helpful reminders for employees.

Seeing that <u>all</u> of the client's non-cleaning specifications, instructions, terms and conditions etc., are carried out to the "letter", or are otherwise adhered to, is very important to establishing and maintaining good customer relations.

Some prime examples are, seeing that all the lighting in the building is left on, or off, after each cleaning, per the customer's instructions, locking exterior and prescribed interior doors as you leave each area for the last time, resetting alarm codes after work has been completed, remembering the disarm code and deactivating the alarm upon entering a facility, in a timely fashion, so as <u>not</u> to trip the alarm and trigger an expensive visit from the police, proper key control (e.g., not losing keys, timely transfer among employees as needed, etc.,), as well as maintaining proper employee identification and compliance with uniform specifications.

Failure to carry out such details, particularly, early on in a customer relationship, will <u>greatly</u>

increase the chances of losing the account. Why?
Because these lapses in service can:

- ***cause the customer money***
  *(e.g., higher electric bills, shorter lighting
  equipment life, police visits, a potential for
  theft and vandalism, etc.);*

- ***put their business operations at risk***
  *(i.e., a potential for theft or vandalism
  through a lapse in security, etc.);*

- ***make employees feel uneasy***
  *(through a perception by an employee, of an
  unsafe work environment after hours, due to
  the potential for theft, or bodily harm, trig-
  gered by the presence of an <u>unidentified</u>
  cleaning service employee);*

- ***undermine credibility and annoy the client***
  *(if employees cannot follow these simple, yet
  vital instructions, human nature dictates that
  "critics" will be quick to pre-judge the cleaning service and cast dispersions on almost
  any other lapse in service, or workmanship,
  perceived or otherwise. This is true of almost
  any service based business, whose services*

229

*can be directly observed by employees or pa-
trons. At some point, the facility administrator will have little choice but to take action
and change cleaning services).*

All of these customer specifications are simple
enough to meet, but may carry with them a near
"zero tolerance" for compliance failures. Proper
training and awareness is essential to ensure that
employees "don't drop the ball". Adding general instructions for such items to a checklist, or
to an employee foldout card, may be a good idea
here. Making stipulations for the performance
of such tasks, a part of the conditions for continued employment, on an employment agreement
or in an employee handbook, for example, may
also provide appropriate incentive for compliance.

Uniforms are an important part of any service or
retail company's image and its identity as well.
Take a moment and reflect on all the instances in
your personal life, where the employees of such
companies are wearing a uniform.

Companies simply would not bear such an expense, or make it a condition of employment,

were it not critical to the image of the company and to the identification of personnel. Uniforms serve as a means of identification and assure the customer's employees and guests, that your company's personnel have a purpose for being present. Cleaning smocks, T-shirts, golf shirts, or hats, etc., should be considered at a minimum. Many uniform companies, provide uniform services to both small and large companies.

In addition, there are many other vendors that can provide cost effective solutions, in the event that uniform services pricing, or a requirement for a minimum number of employees, makes using a uniform manufacturer or service company unfeasible. Some of these companies will even customize a single item, with a lettered insignia or logo.

One such company is **www.embroidered-logos.com**, which will allow you to place an order on-line, for a single item such as a hat, shirt or jacket and have it shipped directly to you. Some other employee uniform resources are:

- **(www.bestu.com)**

- **(www.aramark.com)**

- **(www.cintas-corp.com)**

- **(www.cleanrental.com)**

- **(www.kleenkraftservices.com)**

Some useful techniques that can help your business to maintain good customer relations, borrow from the "age old" sales promotion technique, of leaving some type of remembrance or gift with customer contacts. Not only can you use this approach in conjunction with such sales related activities as onsite consultations, initial cleanings, or following the completion of a service agreement, but also as an ongoing customer relations tool, as well.

For instance, you could leave a gift or remembrance, following the resolution or correction of a serious customer complaint or service related problem, or after the performance of a specialized service such as monthly or quarterly floor care, a deep cleaning etc.,. In fact, if your budget and the profit margin of one or more of your accounts permits, you could leave a remembrance or gift after each performance of a service, or at regular intervals such as weekly, monthly etc.,.

Some ideas for gifts or remembrance are:

- *candy (even as little as several pieces, left regularly, can be a "hit" with customers);*
- *flowers or a single flower in a vase;*
- *nuts;*
- *donuts or pastries;*
- *pens (with your company's name on them);*
- *calendars (with your company's name on them);*
- *fruit & cheese baskets (accompanied by a card addressed from your company);*
- *key chains or rings (with your company's name on them);*
- *tasteful cards or notes, that thank the customer for their patronage and include useful or entertaining information, such as a recipe, general business or consumer facts, humorous or inspirational aphorisms etc.,.*

The appropriate use of this technique, can really enhance the credibility of a small start-up and may help to differentiate your business from competitors, previously employed by your clients.

Chapter 7

Insurance, licenses, taxes, hiring, etc.,

In this chapter, we will discuss various legal and business considerations, that may be of importance to your business, at some point in its development.

Insurance

There are a number of types of business related insurance policies and bonds to consider purchasing, depending on the particular needs of your business. Some types of insurance are mandated by state laws, or may be required in order to win a contract, or to do business with certain clients. Here are some of the basic types of insurance or bonds to consider.

- *Fidelity bonds*
- *Performance surety bonds*
- *General liability insurance*

- *Automobile liability insurance*
- *Workman's compensation insurance*

At a minimum, most cleaning services businesses will need to carry a **fidelity bond**, to protect themselves from liabilities associated with third party claims or lawsuits (e.g., suits filed by your customers, or their employees). Occurrences such as theft, disappearance and destruction, employee dishonesty, fraud, etc., may be covered, depending on the terms and conditions of the bond that is chosen. Many clients will require some proof of bonding for cleaning services employees working in their facilities.

Fidelity bonds can be structured to cover a single employee, or in the form of a blanket bond, covering two or more employees. As with many types of business insurance, these bonds will vary in price and the type of coverage, based on a variety of factors pertinent to your particular business.

The price of the bond will vary, depending on such factors as the amount of coverage (i.e., the total dollar amount that may be reimbursed to your business, in the event of a claim), geographical location, the number of employees involved, specific activities conducted by the employees of the business, the specific types of occurrences that are covered, etc.,. For a single individual, the price of a fidelity bond can be as little as ~$100/ year or more, for $2000-$5000 coverage and ~$325/year or more, for $100,000 coverage. However, rates for fidelity bonds can vary significantly from those mentioned here, based on such factors as geographical area, the number employees under coverage, etc.,.

Some fidelity bond products are tailored by insurance providers to the cleaning industry and are sometime called **janitorial service bonds**. Take the time to understand the terms and conditions of such bonds. Some fidelity bonds require the <u>conviction</u> of a dishonest employee, prior to paying off. Other names sometimes used for fidelity bonds, are third party fidelity bonds and employee dishonesty coverage. It is important to know exactly what occurrences are covered by the bond that you purchase.

It may be necessary to provide fairly detailed information about your business, in order to receive a firm quote for bonds and insurance.

Also, some providers will not supply their insurance products, to companies with a number of employees below a certain threshold, or cut off.

You may find out information about insurance pricing and coverage, through local insurance brokers, specializing in small business coverage, on the internet, or directly from nationally based providers and brokers. Some brokers, providers and search resources, in the area of fidelity and surety bonds, general business liability and other business related insurance, are:

- **(www.insurancenoodle.com)
  on-line quote applications for small business insurance**

- **(www.epolicy.com)
  on-line quote applications for small business insurance**

- **(www.einsurance.com)
  on-line quote applications for small business insurance**

- **Szerlip & Co.,
  (www.szerlip.com)
  1-800-922-0209 endorsed by the NAPC**

- **The Surety Group**
  provides janitorial service bonds
  (www.suretygroup.com)

- **American Bonding Company**
  (www.ambond.com)

- **(www.expresssuretybonds.com)**

- **International Fidelity Insurance**
  (www.ific.com)

- **Zurich NA insurance**
  (zurichna.com)

- **C & A Insurance**

- **The Hartford Insurance Co.**

- **St. Paul Insurance**

- **AIG**

- **Kemper**

- **(www.workmanscompensation.com)**
  on-line quote applications for small business
  insurance

- **(www.ewausau.com)**
  specializes in workman's compensation
  insurance for small business

Performance surety bonds are frequently required in government purchasing bid specifications, for cleaning services contracts. They may also be required by large private concerns. This insurance instrument guarantees 3rd parties (i.e., your customers), that contractors (e.g., your business) will fulfill their obligations in accordance with the terms and specifications of the contract.

Performance bonds are a type of **Contract bond**. Another form of contract bond that is related to a performance bond, is a **Bid bond**, which guarantees that a contractor will provide a performance bond in the event that they win, or bid successfully on a contract.

The small business administration (SBA) has an **Office of Surety Guarantee (OSG)**. This office assists small and minority business in competing with larger companies, for large government contracts, that require hundreds of thousands of dollars of surety bond coverage, by providing guarantees to surety bond provider's "agents", on the behalf of the small or minority contractor. You can find out more at the SBA website, **www.business.gov.**

239

General liability insurance is another very important type of business insurance. This insurance product provides protection for businesses from lawsuits, filed by third parties (e.g., your customers, their employees and their clientele), for occurrences such as bodily injury or property damage.

Automobile liability insurance protects businesses from liabilities, incurred in the event that persons employed by your business, driving company vehicles as authorized, are accused of injury or damage involving a third party. These types of insurance products are also sometimes referred to as **BAP's** (business automobile policies). Some government purchasing bid specifications, for cleaning services contracts, will require the winning contractor to carry a BAP.

Many insurance companies also provide umbrella insurance products, that provide coverage similar or equivalent to, two or more of the above insurance products.

Workman's compensation insurance, or worker's compensation insurance, as it is some times called, is required by state laws for private enterprises operating within their states. A minimum requirement, of few as 1-3 full time employees, may constitute a statutory requirement for businesses to carry workman's compensation insurance. In some cases, part time employees may be entitled to some type of coverage as well. Businesses are not required to provide independent contractors with workman's compensation insurance.

Each state, licenses various insurance carriers to provide workman's compensation insurance. Often, there is a state board of workman's compensation, or a state insurance or labor commissioner, that will provide to employers, guides on workman's compensation requirements. The statutory requirements for this type of insurance will also be provided by licensed insurance carriers in each state. **www.usalawcentral.com**, has excellent links to state government boards, agencies, departments and commissioners and may be a good place to start a search for regulations, guidelines and contacts in your state.

It is a good idea, to consider the advise of a qualified attorney, trustworthy insurance broker, or small business consultant, if you are unsure of how much business insurance coverage you must carry, in cases where it is mandatory. Where it is optional, they can provide advice on the type of insurance products and the amount of coverage, that is best suited to your business.

When insurance is optional, you must weigh the risks versus the benefits of coverage. As with any significant purchasing decision, it is advisable to obtain several quotes, before buying insurance for your business.

Business and occupational licenses

Many states regulate various professions and require a state license to conduct business in their state. The aforementioned internet link to state governments, will lead you to the relevant regulations, business license agencies, departments, or examiners, and is a good place to see if your business is covered by such a statute.

Occupational licenses are required by county and city governments, as a way of generating of revenue and monitoring commerce in their jurisdiction. Occupational licenses may be obtained from the county tax collector, or city hall.

Many counties and some cities will also provide occupational license information and forms on the internet. A typical cost for an occupational business license, starts at ~$50-$100 per year or more, depending geographical location. Additionally, you may have to register with your county, for a **"fictitious business name"**, as required by the Trade Name Registration Act, if the name of your business is other than the name of the owner.

Taxes

There are a number of taxes to consider when operating a business and as with other topics we have presented, a full discussion is outside the scope of this guide. You should consult a qualified tax professional, accountant, lawyer, or the IRS, as well as your state and local tax commissions, in order to ensure that you have educated yourself adequately, regarding all of the requirements and options associated with your business taxes. These professionals can assist you in identifying and understanding federal, state and local tax requirements, planning you tax strategies, and preparing the necessary forms and returns, as well as how to collect, withhold and pay taxes according to mandatory schedules (e.g., quarterly), required for each type of tax that is related to the operation of your business.

The benefits derived from understanding the tax regulations that apply to your business, are the ability to plan your business activities in compliance with the law, the ability to maximize your business deductions or allowances, as well as avoiding unnecessary tax fines or penalties and in a worst case scenario, imprisonment. Additionally, the burden of responsibility for complying with tax regulations, rests with the business owner and not his or her consultants. A brief discussion of some basic small business tax structures, types of taxes, tax forms and several small business tax guides and resources that may be helpful in getting started, are presented here.

Tax structures

The basic business tax structures are shown here.

- *Proprietorships*
- *General Partnerships*
- *Limited liability partnership (LLP)*
- *Limited liability company (LLC)*
- *C corporation*
- *S corporation*

Many individuals starting a cleaning service by themselves, without partners, may find that an individual proprietorship, at least initially, is the most straightforward and the least labor intensive business entity and tax structure to adopt. In fact, it should be noted that the majority of all businesses are sole proprietorships.

The advantages of a **sole proprietorship**, are that one person has complete control (couples will have to choose, who will be the owner and who will be the employee, in this case), the legal requirements are simpler and the cost of implementing the structure, can be as limited as the fees for local business or occupational licenses, which are required, regardless of your business's tax structure.

Sole proprietorships also have fewer legal requirements for dissolution than do partnerships and corporations. The principle disadvantage is that the owner of record, has complete liability for all debts, penalties, lawsuits etc., related to the operation of the business. Additionally, raising capital through the issuance of stock is not an option.

General and limited partnerships are formal legal entities, that involve an agreement among two or more partners. It is usually is drawn up by a qualified attorney, and defines shared authority, responsibilities and liabilities among the partners. In a limited partnership, one or more partners may have <u>limited</u> authority, responsibilities and liabilities. They are consequently called limited partners.

In both cases, the advantages of partnerships often are, an increased capital base (i.e., as provided by the partners), increased intellectual and labor resources, as applicable, as well as a dilution or sharing of liability related to the business's operation. The principle disadvantages may be, shared authority for decision making and shared liability for the debts, penalties and lawsuits etc., generated or caused by actions and activities of other partners, relating to the business or partnership.

An **S corporation** is a business entity and tax structure, that is commonly used to incorporate small business start-ups. It has advantages for limiting liability, sheltering portions of self-employment taxes and raising capital through the issuance of stock. There is a maximum of 75 shareholders. S corporations distribute income through wages and profit distributions.

C corporations pay taxes under standard corporate income tax rules. This structure, is generally used by businesses that are larger in scope than a typical cleaning service start-up. Both S and C corporations have advantages relative to personal liability and avenues for raising capital, but are more expensive and labor intensive to implement and administer. Typically, they are held to a more exacting set of tax rules and reporting requirements, than other business entities. Also, the dissolution of an S or C corporation is more complex, than for other structures.

A **limited liability company** has some of the tax advantages of partnerships and liability protection of a corporation. Owners are called members and they can issue voting and nonvoting stock. It is a relatively new business entity and may be considered as an alternative to other business tax structures.

The IRS provides a wealth of free information on-line such as tax regulations, guides forms, FAQs (i.e., frequently asked questions), etc., that are often downloadable and may also be available on CD, or in booklets, through the website (**www.irs.com**). You can also call, or visit their local offices, to initiate a request, or pick up some guides directly. State and local tax commissions may also provide regulations, tax guides, forms etc., in a similar manner.

A partial list of IRS publications and forms, relevant to federal taxes that may be required for a sole proprietorship, are presented here.

There are also a variety of companies that provide annual business tax return preparation, accounting, payroll services, as well as services for quarterly tax reporting and preparation of employee tax forms and envelopes, for such forms as W-2's and W-3's, etc.,. A short list of the

---

**IRS publications and forms relevant to federal taxes
that may be required for a sole proprietorship:**

Forms and schedules:

- **1040 or 1040-EZ**
  US individual income tax return
  (annual tax return filed by individuals and sole proprietor ships, along
  with a schedule C or C-EZ)

- **1040-ES**
  Estimated tax for individuals
  (form for declaring estimated taxes for the upcoming year)

- **Schedule C or C-EZ**
  profit or loss from a business, or net profit from a business

- **Schedule SE**
  Self employment tax (i.e., equivalent to social
  security and Medicare taxes (FICA taxes), for wage earners, usually
  15.3% of the 1st $76,200 of income)

- **Form 940 or 940-EZ**
  **Employer's annual federal unemployment insurance (FUTA) tax
  return** (a report of all FUTA taxes paid for the year)

- **Form 941**
  Employer's quarterly federal tax return
  (a quarterly report of all of FICA, Medicare taxes withheld from employees for that quarter, (includes employer's FICA contribution))

- **Form 945**
  Annual return of withheld federal income taxes
  (a report of taxes withheld on all non-payroll items such as backup
  withholding, withholding on pensions etc.)

- **Form W-2**
  Wages and tax statements
  (issued to employees each year)

- **Form W-3**
  (needed to transmit copy A of W-2 to the social security administration)

- **Form W-4**
  Employee's tax withholding allowance certificate
  (form documents permission to withhold taxes from wages from employees)

- **Form W-4P**
  Withholding certificate for pensions and annuities

- **Form W-4S**
  Request for federal income tax for sick pay

- **Form W-4V**
  Voluntary withholding request

- **Form W-9**
  (form for requesting social security number (SSN) or Employer identification number (EIN) from parties such as independent contractors, companies, corporations, consultants that you pay, to be entered onto a 1099, for example)

- **Form 1099 and 1096**
  Miscellaneous income
  (used to report miscellaneous income such as resale of greater than or equal to $5,000 of goods, <u>other</u> than in a permanent retail establishment, or payment of greater than or equal to $600 for services performed by non-employees, such as independent contractors, attorneys, accountants, Doctors, etc.,)

- **Form SS-4**
  Application for Employer Identification number
  (form for requesting an EIN for tax purposes)

- **Form SS-8**
  Determination of employee work status for purposes of federal employment taxes and income withholding taxes
  (form that IRS uses in order to determine if a hire is an independent

contractor or an employee for taxation purposes)

- **Form 8109-B and form 8109 booklet**
  Federal tax deposit coupons
  (used to make deposits of for federal withholding from employee's wages, into a bank approved to receive such payments, according to a <u>strict</u> schedule, that can span as little as <u>3 days</u> in any given month)

- **Form 508**
  (filed with authorized financial institution, in conjunction with federal quarterly unemployment insurance deposits for employees)

- **Form 2106 & 2106-EZ**
  Employee Business Expense & Un-reimbursed Employee Business Expense

- **Form 4562**
  Depreciation and Amortization
  (e.g., depreciation of capital equipment)

IRS Publications:
- <u>**Small business tax guide**</u> **(No. 334)**
  (answers to frequently asked questions and instructions for preparing small business taxes)

- <u>**Small business resource guide**</u> **(No. 3207)**

- <u>**Employer's tax calendar**</u> **(No. 509)**
  (calendar for payments, filing and reporting)

- <u>**Information on federal excise tax**</u> **(No. 510)**
  (defines items that may require federal excise taxes on them)

- <u>**Tax withholding and estimating taxes**</u> **(No. 505)** many companies that offer such services, is provided here. Some of these companies will even provide "end to end" services, for a <u>single</u> employee.

Small business tax services

- **(www.paychex.com)**
  end to end payroll and tax reporting services for as few as one employee, to medium sized businesses

- **(www.national-payroll.com)**
  end to end payroll and tax reporting services for small and medium sized businesses

- **(www.payco.com)**
  end to end payroll and tax reporting services small and medium sized businesses

- **(www.buytaxforms.com)**
  provides bulk forms and envelopes for tax reporting

- **(www.adp.com)**
  end to end payroll and tax reporting services for small and medium sized businesses

- **(www.hrblock.com)**
  personal and small business tax services

State taxes

The preparation of state tax returns for businesses, is similar in structure (e.g., income tax, unemployment tax, etc.,), to the preparation of federal taxes and as with your personal income tax preparation, may rely on facts and figures taken from your business's current federal tax return. State taxes may include corporate worth taxes, or ad valorem taxes (i.e., for non-corporate business entities), as well as sales and use taxes (local jurisdictions may also require an additional sales tax). Ad valorem taxes involve an annual tax on the fair market value for a business, typically on the order of 0.5% or less, depending on geographical location.

The collection of sales taxes may be required for the resale of supplies to your clients, should you turn a profit. The eligibility and rules for each type of state and local tax, their collection, payment and reporting, can be obtained on-line, via phone, or by mail, from your state and local governments.

Hiring employees and independent contractors

Just as the performance and success of a winning sports team, is only as good as the sum of the contributions made by each player, so too is the quality of service and success of a commercial or residential cleaning services business. The sum of the contributions of each employee, in any size company and in particular, a small company, is quite likely to be pivotal, both to its initial success and to the continued growth and success of the business.

From the promptness in greeting and providing service to a customer or prospective client, over the phone, to the quality of an initial cleaning, in an attempt to secure a service agreement, to the continued thoroughness and adherence to cleaning specifications and other customer requirements, in the months and years to follow, the performance of every member of the "team" is crucial.

In a professional sports organization, coaches, scouts and general managers, often assist in, or assume the roles of choosing talent for the owner. In a medium to large cleaning services business, a human resources manager along with a line supervisor or manager, might assume these roles.

Its far more common however, owning to limited financial resources, for the owner of a small business start-up, to be making all of the decisions, regarding who will be hired and who might be fired. Entire books have been devoted to the subject of human resources and successful hiring practices, as well as the legal aspects of an employer's responsibility to employees and the rights of employees.

You may wish to research this topic further, both to improve your skills in this area and to ensure that you are in complete compliance with labor laws at all times. At a minimum, you will need to educate yourself, to a number of important factors related to the hiring process, as well as federal, state and local labor laws.

Some of the factors or regulations to consider, are:

- *federal, state and local labor laws regarding*

the employer's responsibilities and the rights of employees;

- *how to establish the right criteria and responsibilities, for any job or position that you wish to fill;*

- *deciding whether and when to hire independent contractors or employees, full and part time;*

- *how to prepare and place effective job ads;*

- *how to interview effectively, run background checks as needed and make competitive offers to the right candidates;*

- *what types of employment agreements or contracts to use;*

- *how to instruct employees and how to motivate employees and maintain happy and productive workers.*

The US department of labor (**www.dol.gov**) and the small business administration or SBA (**www.business.gov**), have a wealth of information on federal labor laws, employer's responsibilities and employees rights, most of which is downloadable directly from their websites, or available by phone, or mail. State labor boards or departments of labor, will have similar information about state requirements and regulations, that are also available through the internet, by phone and by mail. The SBA also has convenient links to state governments on their website.

Two guides that are provided by these agencies for small businesses, are the SBA's <u>Small Business Start-up Kit</u>, and the U.S. department of labor's <u>Small business handbook</u>.

Some of the topics covered, are shown here.

- *federal minimum wage and overtime compensation, under the FLSA or Fair labor Standards Act (currently $5.15/hr and 1.5 times the regular hourly rate, for every hour over 40 hours per week, in the year 2001)*

- *employment eligibility (i.e., rules and requirements for the employment of non-citizens)*

- **employee rights under the FMLA or Family and emergency medical Leave Act**
  (conditions and rules under which employees may take leave from their jobs, for such events as maternity and family medical emergencies)

- **wage garnishment**
  (terms and conditions under which an employees wages may be garnished by creditors and government agencies)

- **OSHA requirements**
  (safety requirement under OSHA and links to that government agency's website)

- **"Workers' rights", for those employees working on federal government contracts**
  (wages, overtime and fringe benefit standards)

- **employee benefit plans**
  (federal regulations regarding voluntary employer pension and benefit plans for their employees)

If and when you set up an office, which houses

employees other than yourself, you will be required to post information regarding several federal and state, labor and safety regulations.

Some of the federally required posters (as applicable), are shown here.

U.S. DOL

- *Federal Minimum Wage & Overtime Poster* (WH-1420)

- *Equal Employment Opportunity (EEO Poster)*

- *Notice to Workers with Disabilities/Special Minimum Wage Poster*

- *Employees Right to a Safe Workplace (OSHA 3165, replaces OSHA 2203)*

- *Log and Summary of Occupational Injuries and Illness (OSHA form 200, must be posted during the month of February)*

- *Notice to Employees Working on Government Contracts Poster (Services Contract*

Act, Walsh-Healy poster, to be posted at government contract worksites)

When you prepare a **job description**, or a written set of responsibilities for a new employee, or a new position, you should keep in mind, what aptitude, education, training and physical requirements might be needed. You should also consider, what level of detail that you will need to provide for an employee's job responsibilities, as well as how that employee will interact with other staff members and customers. Finally, the potential for advancement, should be considered.

Hiring employees
vs
independent contractors

Whether you should hire **full, or part time employees**, or **independent contractors**, is a decision that will have to be made, as you expand your business and prior to withholding and paying payroll taxes and providing benefits. For example, part time employees <u>may</u> be entitled to workman's compensation, but not to unemployment benefits. Independent contractors are generally considered as business entities (i.e., they are in business for themselves) and as such, they are not entitled to either workman's compensation insurance or unemployment benefits, nor do you withhold payroll taxes on them.

The difficulty in hiring independent contractors, or IC's as they are sometimes called, may be in determining and defending their IC status to the IRS and your state tax commission. Typically, you file a 1099 form, for any services that an IC provides for you, that totals $600/year, or more. The IRS provides a four page questionnaire, form SS-8, to determine the status of an employee or IC for tax purposes.

The IRS uses 20 common law factors, to determine whether or not, a person that you hire, is an employee or an IC, for tax purposes. You can view these factors, on-line at the IRS's website (**www.irs.gov**). They weigh several factors against norms for various IC's, and the industries in which they are employed. Failing to meet the criteria for a single factor, does not in and of itself, mean that an individual cannot be classified as an independent contractor.

Some of these factors are:

- *independent contractors, usually cannot be instructed or supervised, as to when, or how to perform a job or tasks* (providing what cleaning, or floor care specifications are involved, may be permissible);

- *generally, employers may not provide tools, equipment, or supplies to independent contractors;*

- *independent contractors, generally do not receive any training from a customer;*

- *independent contractors are generally paid by the job, or on commission, not by the hour, week or month;*

- *the more essential or critical, the involvement of a worker's services are to a business, the more likely the worker is to be classified as an employee, rather than an independent contractor;*

- *independent contractors, generally work for more than one client;*

- *if a worker does not hire and pay his own assistants, then this worker may be considered as an employee, rather than an independent contractor;*

- *working on the hirer's premises, may constitute, an "employer/ employee" relationship.*

For example, If you regularly subcontract an independent floor care specialist company, to perform "turnkey" floor care services, for all of your accounts and you are one, among many of their clients, you should have minimal difficulty in declaring them as independent contractors. This is provided that your business relationship, also meets a sufficient number of the other 20 common law factors, used by the IRS to determine the status of an independent contractor. This type of relationship is similar to a general construction contractor that subcontracts services for electrical, plumbing, sheet rocking, etc.,.

If you use workers from temporary personnel services, for instance, these persons are employees of the temporary services and the temporary service itself becomes your subcontractor. However, if your business is using one or more persons, as "individual" independent contractors, to perform cleaning services, exclusively for you, on a part time basis, you <u>may</u> have a greater burden of proof, in declaring them as independent contractors, as opposed to part time employees.

If you are in doubt, as to whether persons who work for you, will be classified as independent contractors or employees, seek the advice of a qualified tax attorney. This may avoid a potential situation, in which you might have to pay tax penalties and back payroll taxes at the end of the year, for persons reclassified by the government as employees, instead of IC's.

Preparing and submitting job ads

Preparing and submitting **effective job ads**, is a critical part of the hiring process. By selecting the right criteria for candidates and communicating these criteria effectively, in a classified ad, your screening process will be streamlined and receiving responses from a pool of potentially sound candidates, will be more likely.

For example, if you require workers that must

Examples of help wanted ads for
Cleaning services personnel

Janitorial workers needed. Experience preferred but will train. Background check/drug screening. Must have own transportation. Call Acme Janitorial, at xxx-xxx-xxxx, fax resume at xxx-xxx-xxxx, or e-mail resume to e-mail@acmejanitorial.com.

Equal Opportunity Employer

Home cleaning workers needed. Experience not necessary, will train. Background check. Must have own vacuum cleaner and transportation. Call Acme Home Cleaning, at xxx-xxx-xxxx, fax resume at xxx-xxx-xxxx, or e-mail resume to e-mail@acmehomecleaning.com.

Equal Opportunity Employer

Janitorial supervisor wanted. A minimum of 2 years experience required. Background check/ drug screen. Must have own transportation. Call Acme Janitorial, at xxx-xxx-xxxx, fax resume at xxx-xxx-xxxx, or e-mail resume to e-mail@acmehomecleaning.com.

Equal Opportunity Employer

travel quickly to a number of accounts, in a single shift, specify the need for a successful candidate to have their own transportation. If you require employees to provide some of their own cleaning equipment, such as a vacuum cleaner, it will be helpful to include this information in the ad.

Some examples of ads are included here, in order to give you some ideas, as to how you might prepare an effective ad. Ads are most often priced, based on the number of words or lines in the ad, so it is cost effective to keep your ad brief.

Community newspapers, church and apartment complex bulletin boards and some local internet sites, may offer cost free alternatives, to placing paid ads in newspapers with larger circulation. Placing flyers on bulletin boards, that provide free public access, may be a cost effective way of soliciting for potential job applicants. However, the response time may be slower using this approach and the volume of applicants, will most likely be smaller, than for a classified ad in a commercial newspaper.

Interviewing and screening job applicants

Knowing what to look for in an interview, is critical to selecting employees, that will be assets to your business and in keeping turnover to a minimum. Someone who has been employed as a cleaning services worker for a number of years, is more likely to understand what quality of work is necessary to maintain accounts properly and is likely to stay employed with your company longer, provided that they do not have a history of turnover, or extenuating personal circumstances and you offer competitive wages.

This does not mean that persons without cleaning experience are not viable candidates. However, it is necessary to establish with such candidates, an understanding of the nature of the work involved in your business, the consistent quality and precision that are required and where possible, their motivation for seeking employment in cleaning services.

Neat attire, proper grooming, a positive attitude, a clear willingness, or need, to work evenings (as applicable), as well as a respect for, or sense of what type of work is involved and a commitment to quality workmanship at all times, are positive cues to look for in an interview. Ask candidates to provide examples or reasons, as to why you should select them over other applicants and where appropriate, why they have left their most recent positions.

Overly aggressive behavior, "hard sells", a negative tone or attitude, particularly towards previous employers or coworkers, should be evaluated carefully. Candidates displaying such behavior, generally should be avoided. Many people have had some type of difficulty with past employers. However, a display by the candidate, of any behavior or emotion beyond politeness and dispassion, regarding their difficulties or conflicts with previous employers, is frequently a sign, that such problems may continue at future places of employment.

It is a primary rule, touted by most job hunting experts, that job hunters avoid disclosing such information in an interview. If the candidate should volunteer information about difficulties with one or more previous employers, it should be in passing, while explaining their previous work history. If such a disclosure is not followed by a polite declaration of a genuine desire to put these difficulties behind him/ her, free of hostility or sarcasm, the candidate is reliving old hostilities, in what is potentially a new job setting and may not be a good fit for your company.

Background checks and drug screens for successful candidates (i.e., the ones that you intend to hire), are useful, if not necessary precautions to consider, for the protection of your business and the welfare of its existing employees. There are a number of companies that will provide these services at a surprisingly reasonable cost, ranging from as little as ~$10 for a social security number check, ~$20 for a statewide criminal check, ~$12 for a previous employment check and ~$75 for a combined drug screen and background check. Some of the companies which provide these services through the internet, are:

- **(www.accesschecks.com)**

- **(www.hireright.com)**

- **(www.avert.com)**

It is necessary to inform candidates in writing,

that a background check, or drug screen may be performed (this is usually accomplished in a signed employment application and may also be underscored in a classified job advertisement). It is also a requirement to inform the candidate in writing, of any derogatory information that is found and to provide them with a copy. Finally, a formal, written denial of employment (i.e., "adverse action letter") and a copy of the report, must be made available to the candidate.

Employment polices and contracts

You may know through your personal employment experience, whether or not your state is an **"at will state"** (i.e., workers can be dismissed at any time, without citing specified reasons or causes). It may come as news to you, that employees often have certain rights relating to and following termination, regardless of whether your state is an "at will" state, or not.

In any event, you as an employer must be aware of your state's labor laws in this area and how they can affect the way you run your business. In certain situations, the policies in an employer's handbook can be regarded as part of the terms of an enforceable employment contract.

Making a probationary period, a written policy (e.g., in an employee handbook, or employment agreement), such as placing new hires on probation for 90 days, subject to a satisfactory performance review, is quite common in both the public and private sectors. Some employers will also restrict, or withhold certain benefits during part or all this period, as a part of probationary conditions.

Indicating the terms of employment in writing, in an employment agreement or employee handbook, will help protect your rights as an employer. It will also ensure that employees do not labor under a mistaken impression, that they are guaranteed a job for any period of time, unless otherwise specified by a contract.

Employment contracts are an important aspect of hiring, that as an employer, you should be aware of and adequately knowledgeable on. At its roots, a contract between an employer or general contractor and an employee or independent contractor, involves:

- *an <u>offer</u>, made by the employer/ contractor to the prospective employee or independent contractor;*

- *<u>consideration</u>, such as compensation, work responsibilities, work specifications, other terms and conditions, such as benefits etc.;*

- *<u>Acceptance</u>, by the employee or independent contractor.*

Three of the most important types of employment contracts to consider are:

- *general employment contract;*

- *non-compete agreement;*

- *independent contractor agreement.*

A **general employment contract**, will contain the basic contract provisions of an <u>offer</u>, <u>consideration</u> and <u>acceptance</u>. Often, it will also include terms and conditions, that the contracted party (i.e., the employee) acknowledges and agrees to, in signing an agreement and accepting a job offer.

Such provisions, may include a requirement for occasional overtime, availability for 2nd or 3rd shift work, a commitment to the company as their primary employer (i.e., in the event of a scheduling conflict or contractual obligations established with other parties after accepting the contract), stipulations for performance reviews and merit increases, conditions for termination, such as criminal or abusive behavior, use of alcohol or drugs, tardiness, absenteeism, etc.,. Many of these terms and conditions are also frequently documented in an employee handbook.

A statement is often provided in a general employment agreement, that indicates that the employee has been made aware of and will comply with all relevant company policies. You as an employer, have a responsibility to provide such documents to employees at the time of employment, in such cases.

A **non-compete agreement**, is designed to prevent an employee or independent contractor, from stealing your clients out from under you. Typically, they may include the following or similar stipulations:

273

- *a provision stating, that as a condition of employment, the employee or independent contractor will not compete with the company that they are entering into a contract with, upon the termination of their employment or contract, regardless of the cause of termination;*

- *a provision (where applicable), stating that that an <u>employee</u>, or IC, will not directly, or indirectly engage in the same business, or similar businesses that may be in competition with the business that they entering into an agreement with, as named in the contract;*

- *a provision, outlining the <u>area</u> or radius over which the agreement is enforceable and or, the number of <u>years</u> for which the agreement is enforceable.*

If for example, you should employ free lance home or janitorial cleaners, or floor care specialists (i.e., independent contractors), you may need to modify or clarify the 2nd stipulation presented above. You may wish to word this stipulation, so as to allow the independent contractor to conduct the same type of business, but not with your present or recent clients (e.g., stipulating a period of time, such as one to three years, over which this is enforceable), or if they are amenable, within the area that your business or clients are located.

Some employment agreements include "Confidentiality and ownership" stipulations, requiring confidentiality, or indicating that any creative processes such as inventions, and business processes developed by an employee or independent contractor, while in the service or employ of an employer/ contractor, in which they have entered into an agreement with, are the property of that employer or contractor. It should be noted, that non-compete agreements can be successfully contested, when they can be shown to prohibit a person from earning a living.

Independent contractor agreements, may include some of the same provisions and stipulations found in general employment and non-compete agreements. Some of the important distinctions between an independent contractor agreement and other business contracts (i.e., general employment and non-compete contracts), are:

- *independent contractor agreements use a title (i.e., such as "Independent Contractor Agreement") and language, that clearly distinguish them, as being applicable to a contracting party (i.e., your business) and an independent contractor. The use of the terms "employee" and "employer" are <u>avoided</u> for this reason;*

- *the scope of work or tasks are defined and work specifications are often enumerated or referenced;*

- *the length or period of time, over which the contracting agreement is enforceable, is usually defined in terms of completion of a specific set of tasks, over a <u>finite</u> period of time, beginning on a specific date and ending on a specific date. Stipulations for termination of the contract, such as a 30 day notice for termination, due to unsatisfactory performance, or a more stringent stipulation, such as immediate termination for unsatisfactory work, may also be made;*

- *consideration or payment stipulations, usually require the independent contractor to present an <u>invoice</u> to the contracting party, at the completion of service, or at prescribed intervals; with a finite grace period for payment.*

Additionally, some independent contracting agreements will provide an **indemnity clause**, which protects the contracting party from harm, expense or liability, caused by the actions of, or attributed to the independent contractor. Still other independent contracting agreements, will include language, that speaks to one or more of the common law factors used by the IRS to define independent contractors.

Such language, usually provides some additional protection for the contracting party against breach of contract, liabilities and clarifies the responsibilities of the contracting party and the independent contractor. It also seeks to demonstrate further, that the <u>contracted</u> party (i.e., the independent contractor), is not an employee of the contracting party.

An example of such language, is a provision or

clause, that declares that the independent contractor will not be provided with health insurance, unemployment insurance, workers compensation insurance, etc.,. Another example of such stipulations, is that the independent contractor will provide their own tools and supplies.

There are many government, commercial and nonprofit websites, which provide examples of general employment, non-compete and independent contractor agreements. Some of these are <u>copyrighted</u>, while others are not copyrighted. A few of these resources are provided here, so that readers can familiarize themselves with the terms and language used in such agreements.

Sources for sample employment contracts

• **(www.digital-women.com)**

• **(www.legaldocs.com)**

• **(www.lawsmart.com)**

• **(www.allbusiness.com)**

• **(www.lectlaw.com)**

Having an attorney, qualified in labor or contract law, review any agreement that you legally copy, modify, or draw up entirely by yourself, is always advisable. Unless you, or someone you know and trust, is competent in contract and labor laws, as well as in drawing up employment agreements, you may not be able to ensure that such agreements are enforceable, in compliance with federal and state laws and adequately protect your business from unforeseen liabilities.

Small business legal services

There are most likely, a number of qualified attorneys where you live, that may be of assistance to you in many aspects of your business, including, tax preparation, writing and reviewing contracts, representing you in the event of litigation, as well as providing you sound advice, for compliance with federal state and local laws, applicable to your business (e.g., tax and labor laws).

There are also a number of reputable legal services, available through the internet, that will provide such services as:

- *cost effective legal insurance coverage*

(note: terms of coverage may be limited, as stipulated by the insurance carrier);

- ***on-line legal services** (e.g., such as legal record searches);*

- ***free legal advice** (this advice is not intended to replace professional legal counsel, where it is necessary, or appropriate);*

- ***phone consultation** (usually as a part of a packaged service, or pre-paid insurance plan);*

- ***third party letters and phone calls** (on the behalf of your business);*

- ***collection letters** (i.e., for collection of payments owed to your business);*

- ***paid legal counsel** (e.g., pre-trial and trial litigation).*

Some insurance providers, such as **Pre-paid legal Services Inc.**, provide limited insurance coverage for various services, as mentioned above, for individuals, families and businesses, starting as low as ~$15-$25/ month, or more. Some internet resources for legal services or general advice are listed here.

- **(www.prepaidlegal.com)
  legal insurance coverage for individuals**

- **(www.companycounsel.com)
  provides legal services for small companies**

- **(www.pocketlawyer.com)
  pre-paid legal services**

- **(www.lawstreet.com)
  provides free legal advice from lawyers as
  well as other legal information services**

- **(www.freeadvice.com)
  legal advice bulletin board and chat room
  forum**

Motivating and maintaining employees

Motivating and maintaining employees, is no easy task and as with many of the topics in this guide, entire books, management seminars and training courses are devoted to this subject. A few maxims, or precepts are shown here, that may provide the novice employer/ entrepreneur with a "starting point", or frame of reference.

- *Be interested, but not always directly involved*

- *Lead by example, but not in a showy or trivial manner*

- *Listen to employees and teach them to listen carefully to the concerns of customers*

- *Learn when to delegate and how to delegate effectively*

- *Cultivate genuine pride in quality workmanship and consistency, that is so vital, not only to the success of a cleaning business, but to any enterprise*

- *Instill in your employees, a pride and an identity, in being a valued member of your company and in the importance of representing the company at all times, to the mutual benefit and continued success of both the company and its employees*

- *Provide competitive compensation, incentives and rewards, to motivate employees to grow to their potential and ensure the continued success of the business*

- *Develop the insight to recognize when a "business to business", or an "employer to employee relationship", is harmful to your business and or, to the morale and welfare of your employees and then have the courage to take appropriate and decisive action*

Additional research and study is strongly urged. As with most skills we acquire, proficiency at motivating and maintaining employees comes with experience and also with the careful selection of employees, competitive compensation and a little luck.

Chapter 8

After the first reading

Research

You are enthusiastically invited, to review and research further, each of the major topics presented in this resource guide. Towards that end, the resources mentioned throughout the guide, have been compiled into some 11 pages, indexed by topic and in the order that they appeared in the text.

Research using these resources, will also serve to underscore and illustrate or animate, the discussion of each topic presented in this guide, as well as, help to answer many of the reader's questions, that have either arisen, or may have been left unanswered upon a first reading.

Spending several hours, earnestly exploring these resources, in relation to one's individual or specific needs, will prove invaluable to any reader making the decision to start their own

cleaning business. A minimum of 16-24 hrs research to start, is suggested for the serious
minded aspiring entrepreneur, who has limited
experience in cleaning services, or in starting a
business (e.g., devote a few of weekends to your
initial research).

Finally, many of the internet resources provided,
may be used directly and immediately to:

- *establish relationships with cleaning services professionals and pertinent small business services;*

- *purchase equipment, supplies, advertising
  and business insurance;*

- *initiate advertising campaigns and marketing research;*

- *serve as business research tools that can be
  useful not only initially, but <u>continually</u> as
  your business grows.*

"Working smart", and building on success

Once you make that all important decision to prepare a business plan and commit your time and financial resources, there are a few practical approaches that are worth considering as you proceed. To begin with, temper your enthusiasm with realistic expectations and focus most of your energies towards small goals, that will help you build your business, in a calculated and "sure footed" manner.

Avoid acting on impulse and relying on blind hopes. Anticipate how each goal will be funded and or, accomplished and how the completion of each goal will contribute to the solvency and growth of your business.

"Affirmation without action is delusion"
- Anthony Robbins

Consider developing plans or strategies that conserve your financial resources, so that you always have reserves, to use in case of emergencies and as a basis for funding the future growth of your business. Avoid unnecessary debt or expenditures, whenever possible.

For example, if you do not yet, have appropriate transportation and you have decided that you need to acquire a vehicle such as a truck, SUV, or van, consider buying a reliable late model, used vehicle, as opposed to a new vehicle. Depending on your situation and personal finances, you may wish to trade your current vehicle, in order to conserve your resources further. The same goes for other major equipment purchases.

Consider purchasing demonstrator models, or reliable used floor care equipment, instead of new equipment. You may wish to set a goal, of initially renting floor care equipment and applying the profits of "one time" floor care jobs, towards the purchase of your own equipment. A similar approach can be applied to other types of cleaning equipment, such as pressure washers, etc.,.

Make each purchase of equipment and supplies, a cost effective contribution to the growth of your business. **Avoid fancy or frivolous purchases, based on emotion, or the allure of a prestigious image** (e.g., fancy furniture or computers, extravagant and expensive advertising or websites, or infrequently used gadgets, etc.,).

If you are new to cleaning services and your long term goal is to be a full time janitorial contractor, consider training yourself and building your financial resources, by working part time for one or more cleaning services, while maintaining your existing primary job.

Once you have adequate experience, business contacts and financial resources, then you can consider working full time as a contractor. You should also have enough clients lined up, to sustain the business and pay your personal bills, once you make the switch. This "bootstrap" approach, has been used successfully, by countless individuals making the transition from working for an employer, to working for themselves. The same approach can be applied to other cleaning business ventures, such as floor care or window washing services.

To minimize personal economic risk, you may want consider maintaining a part time job in your present field (as applicable), once you have made the commitment to a full time cleaning service venture. The additional income can be used to assist in the transition, providing emergency financial reserves, in the event of unforeseen events, such as losing a major account or expenses for major equipment repair or replacement, as well as to provide financial fuel for the expansion of your business.

Adaptability and consensus based decisions

Finally, as you plan your strategies and seek out the advice and information needed to reach your business goals, try to base your major decisions on a consensus from more than one reliable source, wherever possible. Then thoughtfully and carefully adapt what you have learned, to your particular situation.

What works in one situation, may not work or apply in another situation. The more <u>reliable</u> sources that you the draw information from, the greater the probability that you will find essential <u>details</u>, relating to your particular situation. Consequently, you are more likely to make decisions, that best suit your current situation and contribute effectively to the achievement of your long term goals.

"A goal that is properly set, is halfway reached"
- Zig Ziglar

Resources

Internet search resources:

- (ww.w.searchenginewatch.com)

Resources for preparing a business plan:

- Small Business Administration's
  "The business plan road map to success"
  (www.irs.gov/smallbiz provides a
  link to a free downloadable PDF file)

- (www.nolo.com)
  (search for "small business" in the
  encyclopedia search engine)

- Business Planning Center
  (www.businessplans.org)

- www.bplans.com
  (provides planning tools and sample
  business plans)

- Yahoo! small business directory
  (search for "business plans")

Copyright and Tradename search resources:

- (www.legalname.com)

- (www.loc.gov/copyright)
  (U.S. copyright office/ library of congress website)

- www.uspto.gov
  (U.S. patent and trademark office)

Floor care resources:

Floor & Carpet Care
  ($19.95 at 877-662-6905 or
  www.janitorbooks.com)

- www.hillyard.com
  (excellent instruction booklets
  available for use with their strip and wax
  and carpet care products)

- www.etcpads.com
  (has strip and wax guidelines on-line,
  for use in conjunction with their scrubbing
  and buffing pads)

- Stone and Ceramic Tile Floor Care
  free downloadable maintenance guides
  (www.aquamix.com or 800-366-6877 for
  technical assistance)

- Hardwood , Carpet & Vinyl Floor Care
  free downloadable maintenance guides
  (www.profloor.com or 800-281-EASY)

- Floor Facts & Carpet Stain Guide
  (www.bissell.com)

- Chemical Information & Stain Guides
  For The Professional Carpet Cleaning
  Industry (www.bane-clene.com)

- (www.cmmonline.com)
  (provides articles on cleaning & cleaning

industry news)

- Glossary of Hard Floor Care
  (www.coastwidelabs.com)

- IICRC and NAPC websites

- (www.topfloor.com)

Janitorial equipment and supply websites:

- (www.cleanking.com)

- (www.janitorialsuppliesstore.com)

- (www.jani-mart.com)

- (www.fishmansupply.com)

- (www.1st-janitorial-equipment-and-supplies.com)

- (www.cleanproindustries.com)

- (www.coastalpapersupply.com)

- (www.cleaning-equipment.com)

- (www.centaur.machines.com)

- www.nycoproducts.com

- (www.janitorshop.com)

- (www.bigtray.com)

- (www.cyberclean.com)

Resources for contacting professional cleaners:

- (www.cleaningassociation.com)
  National Association of professional cleaners (NAPC)

- (www.cleanlink.com)
  cleaning articles links and bulletin board

Advertising resources:
- www.usps.com
  (U.S. Post Office website, post card and package mailing services)

- Val-Pak®
  (neighborhood mailer service)

Links to state government websites:

- (www.pagevendor.com)

- (www.usalawcentral.com)

- (www.business.gov)

Resources for further research on bidding, price structures, production rates and work loading:

- Cleaning management Institute
  (articles & resources on cleaning)
  (www.cmmonline.com)
  1-518-783-1281

- Building Service Contractors Association International
  The Official BSCAI Guide to Bidding & Estimating
  (www.bscai.org or www.amazon.com (~$60)

- Industry facts, figures and Trends
  Donald E. Tepper, at (www.amazon.com) (~$160)

- The NAPC Guide to Estimating Cleaning Services
  (www.cleaningassocation.com)

- Bidding and Estimating Janitorial Contracts
  (www.janitorbooks.com)

- (www.janitorialbidding.com)
  sells books on bidding

- Rim Rock Technologies software
  at their website or (www.cleanpro.com)
  bidding and bidding proposal software

- NAPC bulletin board
  (www.cleaningassociation.com)

- (www.cleanlink.com) forum/bulletin board

- (www.windows101.com)
  bulletin board & specialty window
  cleaning equipment & supplies

- (www.window-cleaning-net.com)
  bulletin board

Resources for cleaning practices and techniques and training:

- The Cleaning Encyclopedia
  (a professional guide to cleaning
  everything from A-Z), Don Aslett,
  ~$6.29 at (www.amazon.com)

- (www.doityourself.com)
  cleaning tips and cleaning forum

- (www.frugalitynetwork.com)
  provides links to house cleaning tips

- <u>Clean your house safely and effectively</u>:
  <u>without harmful chemicals</u>, Randy Dunford,
  ~$9.95 at (www.opengroup.com)

- The IEHA, International Executive Housekeepers
  Association (www.ieha.org)
  provides certification and registration for
  institutional cleaners and supervisors

- <u>500 Terrific ideas for cleaning everything</u>:
  expert advice from choosing supplies to cleaning
  absolutely everything, Don Aslett, ~$6.95 at
  (www.opengroup.com)

- (www.goclean.com) Mary Findley's
  Cleaning tips and monthly newsletters
  related to cleaning

- <u>Cleaning performance handbook</u>
  Gary Clipperson at (www.nationalproclean.com)

- (www.about.com) focus on PC support
  cleaning tips for cleaning PC's, without
  damaging them

- (www.a2zcarpet.com)
  carpet care guide, stain removal guide

Resources for employee safety information and training:

- (www.osha.gov)
  (Occupational Safety and Health Administration)

- Handbook for Small Businesses
  (OSHA publication 2209)

- Hazard Communication Guideline
  for Compliance
  (OSHA publication 3111)

- Keeping Your Workplace Safe
  (OSHA brochure-flyer)

- Assessing the Need for Personal Protection Equipment (A
  Guide for Small Business Employers)
  (OSHA publication 3151)

- Chemical Hazard Communication
  (OSHA publication 3084)

- Personal protective Equipment
  (OSHA publication 3077)

- Small Businesses– Questions & Answers
  (OSHA publication 3163)
- (www.msdsonline.com)

- (www.msdssearch.com)

- (www.chesnet.com)

- (www.free-training.com)

- (www.natlenvtrainers.com)

Resources for employee uniforms:

- (www.embroidered-logos.com)

- (www.cintas-corp.com)

- (www.cleanrental.com)

- (www.kleenkraftservices.com)

Resources for business insurance and bonding:

- (www.insurancenoodle.com)
  on-line quote applications for small business
  insurance

- (www.epolicy.com)
  on-line quote applications for small business
  insurance

- (www.einsurance.com)
  on-line quote applications for small business
  insurance

- Szerlip & Co.,
  (www.szerlip.com)
  1-800-922-0209
  endorsed by the NAPC

- The Surety Group
  provides janitorial service bonds
  (www.suretygroup.com)

- American Bonding Company
  (www.ambond.com)

- (www.expresssuretybonds.com)

- International Fidelity Insurance

(www.ific.com)

- Zurich NA insurance
  (zurichna.com)

- C & A Insurance

- The Hartford Insurance Co.

- St. Paul Insurance

- AIG

- Kemper

- (www.workmanscompensation.com)
  on-line quote applications for small business
  insurance

- (www.business.gov)
  SBA's Office of Surety Guarantee (OSG)

Resources for business related taxes:

- (www.irs.gov)
  Internal Revenue Service website

- (www.paychex.com)
  end to end payroll and tax reporting services for as few as one
  employee, to medium sized businesses

- (www.national-payroll.com)
  end to end payroll and tax reporting services for small and medium sized businesses

- (www.payco.com)
  end to end payroll and tax reporting services

small and medium sized businesses

- (www.buytaxforms.com)
  provides bulk forms and envelopes for tax reporting

- (www.adp.com)
  end to end payroll and tax reporting services for small and medium sized businesses

Resources for labor laws and employee rights in the work place:

- (www.dol.gov)
  The US department of labor

- (www.business.gov)
  the small business administration or SBA

Resources for employee background cheeks and drug screening:

- (www.accesschecks.com)

- (www.hireright.com)

- (www.avert.com)

Sources for sample employment contracts:

- (www.digital-women.com)

- (www.legaldocs.com)

- (www.lawsmart.com)

- (www.allbusiness.com)

- (www.lectlaw.com)

Resources for legal services:

- (www.prepaidlegal.com)
  legal insurance coverage for individuals
- (www.companycounsel.com)
  provides legal services for small companies

- (www.pocketlawyer.com)
  pre-paid legal services

- (www.lawstreet.com)
  provides free legal advice from lawyers as well as other legal information services

- (www.freeadvice.com)
  legal advice bulletin board and chat room forum

Index

advertising 85-134
advertising strategies 105-106
advertising, "cold calling" 130-133
advertising, "door to door" 130-133
advertising, classified 118
advertising, components 107
advertising, internet 121-127
advertising, local radio 128-130
advertising, local television 128-130
advertising, signs/ lettering 131
advertising, license plates 131

background checks 267-268
bid bonds 237
bid estimating 138-149
bid estimating factors 136-138
bid proposal, example 187-190
bid proposal, preparation 180-190
bidding formulas 138-149
bidding requirements 161-170
bidding specifications 161-170
bloodborne pathogens 221-222
bonnet carpet cleaning 64-65
breakeven formula 50
brochures 118-119
brooms 71-72
bucket & wringers 72-73
burnishers 67-71
business cards 117-118
business interactions 133-134
business licenses 240-241
business plan 27-50
business plan checklist 29-30
business tax services 249-250

C corporation 245

carpet extraction 62-64
carpet extractors 62-66
carpet shampooing 64
cleaning ergonomics 77-78
cleaning practice, examples 211
cleaning practices 203-213
cleaning specifications, example 165-168
cleaning supplies 79-85
client negotiations 191-202
company name/ logo 30
competition, assessing the 99-105
consumer complaints 223
contract bonds 237
contract, general employment 270-271
contract, independent contractor 273-277
contract, non-compete 271-273
copyright search 32
customer relations 222-231
customer relations, basics 224-225
customer surveys 114-116

direct mailing data bases 113-114
distribution of overhead 148-149
door hanger, example 110-111
door hangers 108-111
drug screens 267-268
dust mops 71-73

employment contracts 268-277
employment policies 268-277
equipment 51-84
exposure control 221

fictitious business name 241
fidelity bonds 233
floor care equipment 52-72
floor machines 66-71
flyer, example 94-95

flyers 89-95
franchises 18

gifts and remembrances 229-232
governments contracts 161-170

hard floor care equipment 66-73
hiring employees 252-281
home cleaning clientele 86-87
home cleaning services 42-43
home page, example 127
housekeeping carts 75-76

IC's, common law factors 259-262
independent contractors, IC's 258-262
insurance 232-241
insurance, automobile 238
insurance, general liability 238
insurance, workman's compensation 239
internal revenue service 249-250
internet search pointers 19-21
interviewing and hiring 265-268
introduction 4
IRS publications & forms 247-249

janitor caddies 75-76
janitor carts 75-76
janitorial cleaning services 43-44
janitorial services clientele 87
job ads, examples 263

labor regulations 254-258
labor, US dept. of 254-258
laser ultrasonic estimator 152-153
legal insurance 277-279
limited liability company 246

mailers, neighborhood 117

marketing 85-134
meta tags 124-125
MSDS sheets 220-221

NAPC (national association of professional cleaners) 100
NOA, example 165-168
notice of awards (NOA's) 161-170

occupational licenses 240-241
OSHA   214-215

partnerships 244-245
PDCA cycle 15-16
performance surety bonding 237
post card mailer 112-116
PPE 221
preparing a business plan 27-50
preparing job ads 262-264
price per square foot, (per month, per year) 169
price per square foot, charts 174-177
price structure, home cleaning 160
price structure, janitorial 44
print advertising media 108-127
production rate charts 174-176
production rates, determining 150-155

resources, internet 288-298

S corporation 245
safety measures 216-219
safety practices 214-222
safety regulations 216
SBA, office of surety guarantee (OSG) 237-238
shampooing machines 64, 66
Shewart's PDCA cycle 15-16
small business legal services 277-279
small cleaning tools/ aids 78-79
sole proprietorship 243-244

state taxes 251
supplies 51-84

target market 37, 96-99
targeted advertisement 40
tax structures 243-251
tax, ad valorem 251
tax, corporate worth 251
taxes 241-251
team based cleaning 211-213
trademark search 32

uniforms 228-229
universal precautions 222

vacuum cleaners 57-62
virtual phone numbers 121

website home page 123
website preparation 124-126
website submission 124-126
wet mops 71-73
work loading 156-157
work loading, example 156

yellow pages 119-121

About the Author:

Walter Fenix is a veteran of several business start-ups, with over 20 years experience in business and technical management. Mr. Fenix develops business tools including guides, manuals and software for use by small businesses and independent contractors. Other titles by Walter Fenix and offered through the Knouen Group include:

Cleaning Services Bid Estimation:
A Resource Guide To Cleaning Services Bid Estimating, Work
Loading And Cost Accounting
(Suggested retail price $69.95 US)

Janitorial & Home Cleaning Services:
Bid Estimating Worksheets For Microsoft Excel*
(Suggested retail price $39.95 US)
*** Software CD**

To learn more about these titles and how to order them individually, or at deep discounts through special package offers visit:

www.janitorial-and-home-cleaning-business-systems.com

or send an e-mail to:

email@janitorial-and-home-cleaning-business-systems.com

Book and software publications from the Knouen Group can also be purchased through many major on-line book retailers

THE KNOUEN GROUP

CPSIA information can be obtained at www.ICGtesting.com
Printed in the USA
LVOW082133140212

268669LV00001B/146/P